A THOUSAND INVISIBLE CORDS

An American Lawyer's Unorthodox Journey

SANFORD H. PERLISS

ISBN: 0615592260
ISBN-13: 9780615592268

To Sallie and Bob Perliss, Jia-Ning and our children

Author's Note

In relating my career as an attorney, I have been vigilant to keep client identity confidential and to safeguard privileged communications. I have also been careful not to reveal anything that would be hurtful to anyone. I have therefore changed most names (using pseudonyms), ages, genders, ethnicities, locations, dates, places and other identifying details. In cases where a client is described, aspects of the client's appearance, characteristics, history, attributes and mannerisms have been thoroughly altered. Since clients' identifying features have been changed, it is quite likely that any resemblance to real persons, living or dead, is purely coincidental. Most of the stories in this book concluded over ten years ago, many more than twenty years ago and some as far back as twenty-five. Both the chronology and circumstances of events are intentionally obscured. In addition to my opinions, observations and experiences, this book includes cases as well as principles of law. Individuals should not rely on the general legal principles written in this book. One should always obtain legal advice to address his or her unique situation.

TABLE OF CONTENTS

Chapter IV: Adrenaline Overdose: DUI, Drugs & Domestic Violence   77

Chapter V: Human Vice: Slavery, Trafficking & Sex Workers   105

Chapter VI: Breaking and Entering the Global Cookie Jar: Theft & Fraud   129

Chapter VII: Growing & Evolving: Merging Criminal and Immigration Law   165

Introduction
American Lawyer for the Chinese

*When we try to pick out anything by itself, we find that
it is bound fast by a thousand invisible cords that cannot
be broken, to everything in the universe*
— John Muir

"It doesn't happen like this in China," she said wiping the tears from her cheeks. She had no idea her 911 call would have such devastating consequences. In California, when police respond to a domestic violence call, they *will* make an arrest. In China, the police are more likely to mediate the dispute. Now, she must hire an attorney and pay a bail bondsman $5,000 to post the $50,000 bond. When the dispute between spouses is about money, the arrest of one puts added pressure on the financial health of the marriage. Domestic violence prosecutions highlight a common Chinese immigrant misperception of American legal procedures. Once a spouse is arrested, both spouses suffer. She was worried sick about her husband now in jail and agonized how she would survive without him. She hired me. I practice law in the Los Angeles Chinese community.

My clients often inform me that in China, enforcement of the law is flexible and forgiving. This contrasts with the widespread American perception of the Chinese legal system as harsh. In an ordinary neighborhood in China, cultural and social intercourse is generally humane and civilized with regard to petty criminal and non-political matters. In a shoplifting case in China, one may be required to return the stolen goods and be counseled. He or she would not be prosecuted as here in the United States. In China, a dispute could be resolved through a family or friend's connection with someone in authority.

In the United States, the average Chinese is a model citizen: hardworking, family-oriented and law-abiding. There is time for friends and leisure activities, ensuring a balanced and healthy individual and society. The crime rate among Chinese is very low. I happen to work with that small percentage of Chinese who do get into legal trouble. I advise my clients that America is a land of law. The fact that one is a good person may not help when legal problems arise; he or she will be treated the same as anyone else. There is no bribery, no *guanxi* (relationship) that can make things happen. I encourage my Chinese clients to spend time learning the fundamentals of our system of law. Be wary of lawyers who, appealing to a Chinese cultural understanding of law, suggest they have *guanxi* and can use their influence to extricate a client from trouble.

By sharing my experiences and cases, my goal is to inspire immigrants to understand the consequences of violating the law in their adopted homeland. Some in the immigrant community do not recognize the gravity of certain deeds. They may think their behavior is legal, or consider an action so minor that nobody would care. American society tends to be unforgiving. Immigrants must understand they are living in this social atmosphere of strict application of the law. It is essentially a fair system, but it is likewise affected by human weakness and prejudice.

Often new immigrants have little understanding of the individual rights they inherit upon arrival in the United States. These fundamental rights are found in the United States Constitution and apply to each individual, citizen or not. Pertaining to everyday criminal law and procedure, our rights include access to and representation by a lawyer, to be free from unreasonable search and seizure, to bail, to a speedy and public jury trial, to confront and cross-examine witnesses, to testify on one's own behalf or remain silent, and to use the subpoena power of the court's process to compel witnesses to appear in court.

In America, these rights are inviolable, but they do not guarantee a favorable result, only a relatively fair process. In the legendary court case, *Miranda vs. Arizona*, the Supreme Court ruled law enforcement must advise suspects of their constitutional rights during a custodial interrogation. American popular culture has embraced this concept and a viewer can watch actors reading Miranda rights to suspects on television dramas every night. Throughout my career, clients have told me, "The police did not read me my rights." The client therefore expects I should easily get the case dismissed. I tell the client he is mistaken. The failure of the police to read one's rights is only relevant to the admissibility of the client's un-Mirandized statement. The remedy for failing to Mirandize a suspect is the suppression of the statement the suspect gave, not dismissal of the charges. In other words, the un-Mirandized statement cannot be received into evidence against the defendant. However, the testimony of the twenty witnesses, who watched the defendant stab the victim to death, will be admitted.

In this memoir, I recount my journey from deputy district attorney to criminal defense lawyer in the multicultural melting pot of Los Angeles; from well-known criminal and immigration lawyer in the Chinese communities of the San Gabriel Valley to pioneering American attorney practicing law in China; and finally, from son of Midwestern Jewish American middle class parents to a son-in-law of Taiwan and the People's Republic of China. The accounts that follow have taken place over the course of my career and are presented in the hope the reader will enjoy a rich variety of cases, and in so doing, learn essentials of US law. I have handled thousands of cases. This book only presents a sampling. Of these, most are brief descriptions of facts and outcomes, not in-depth legal analyses. Some cases are quite unusual, a handful even famous. Some occurred while I was a prosecutor, most after I entered private practice as a criminal defense and immigration lawyer. The two stories in Chapter I highlight how seemingly minor errors of judgment caused major problems for otherwise model citizens. Chapter II outlines my early legal career in the District Attorney's Office. Chapters III through VI describe thought-provoking criminal cases, loosely organized by categories of crimes. Chapter VII merges a criminal and immigration law practice, and in Chapter VIII, horizons broaden, and suddenly I am traveling and practicing law overseas. You will see the serendipity of odd interconnections. A "thousand invisible cords" link together both events in my life and our conversation.

Chapter I

Even Model Citizens
Encounter Legal Trouble

On a January dawn 2001, as the golden sun illuminated the serene San Gabriel Mountains, the valley below was awakening. The final stages of Operation Auto Injury swept through the Chinese community. Shaken from their sleep that chilly morning by the shock of armed officers, scores of suspects were arrested for insurance fraud. Their loved ones wept as they were handcuffed and taken to jail. Since it was a Thursday, if bail could not be posted, the earliest they could be brought to court was the following Monday. Later, attorneys on the case speculated that law enforcement deliberately chose the end of the week to keep those arrested in custody as long as possible, at least over the weekend. It was the first time most of these ordinary, hard-working, family-oriented people were in trouble.

The District Attorney's Fraud Division, in cooperation with the California Department of Insurance, had conducted a yearlong sting. DA investigators, along with sheriffs and local police, fanned out across the San Gabriel Valley to make these arrests. The massive arrests were reported in the local media,

1

including all five San Gabriel Valley Chinese newspapers. Those arrested "lost face" by the publication of their names and were overtaken by fear of the unknown and a possible protracted legal process with serious punitive consequences.

The arrestees were victims of legitimate car accidents. They had real injuries and were being treated at the same Chinese chiropractic clinic, where the District Attorney's Office had planted an undercover officer. The officer's job was to feign cooperation with unscrupulous "law offices" to have patients agree to increase their insurance demands by fabricating doctor visits in excess of the actual treatment. The undercover officer, an attractive woman, had a pleasant, polite and soft-spoken manner, easy to get along with, *easy to agree with*. She was warm and welcoming, as if she were inviting you to a cup of tea. While of Chinese descent, she spoke only English. As a pretext, she held the position of billing representative. The patients trusted her. How would they know the truth?

At each chiropractic visit, the patient would sign a form, proof that he or she had appeared for therapy. The forms were used to determine the extent, and therefore cost of the treatment, establishing the basis for the damages claimed against the insurance companies. The accident victims believed the chiropractor was their friend, providing the needed therapy. Although surreptitiously working with the DA's Office, the chiropractor was genuinely helping to restore their health. Most were suffering from soft tissue injury, which commonly heals in three to four months. They would receive therapy and assume that would be the end of it. The chiropractor would prepare a report documenting the extent of the treatment and resulting costs. The report would be sent to the "law office," which would write a letter to the insurance company demanding exaggerated monetary damages based on the chiropractor's report.

Many of the patients thought they had hired legitimate law offices and reputable lawyers to file their claims. In reality, most were represented by sham law offices run by managers, often unaffiliated with a lawyer. At the end of the treatment, the patient would be called by either the chiropractor's office or the law office manager. Patients would be told they needed to work out the final bill with the chiropractor's office. The law office manager, unaware of the sting operation, would talk to the "billing representative" to arrange an appointment for the patient to finalize the bill. The undercover agent used a small office in the clinic where a hidden camera captured the patient settling his or her account. The officer would say, "Do you know why you are here?" Some knew, some did not. Several said they were just there to settle their bill. In certain cases, language was a problem. The undercover officer might say, "You were treated only fifteen times for a total of $2,400. If you were treated twenty-four times, the bill would be $3,500. You would earn more money from the insurance company. If you fill out ten more of these forms, we could bill for more money." Then the undercover investigator would gently place the forms in front of the patient for his or her signature. Many patients asked if they could get into trouble. They were reassured by the affable undercover officer that as long as they did not tell anyone, it would be all right. The crime did not originate in the mind of the patient, yet many went along with the conspiracy. These patients were collateral damage in the DA's pursuit of the law office managers.

The patients arrested were charged with two felonies: preparing and submitting a fraudulent insurance claim. The case was broken down into five indictments, categorized by which of the five law offices the patient had used. Some of the managers had advertised they were working for a law firm. In fact, only two real lawyers were minimally involved in the case, involving just a handful of clients.

The DA's Office secured an indictment from the grand jury based on thousands of pages of testimony. There were videotapes of most patients settling the final bill. The case was sent to Judge Orton's courtroom in downtown Los Angeles. Judge Orton is an experienced, smart judge, so I was confident the massive case would be resolved fairly. Most of the defendants still in custody were released O.R. (own recognizance), meaning they were released on their promise to return to court. They were free, but their worries were not over. This case would take a long time, as there were many defendants and many lawyers. Each defendant had the right to his or her own attorney. However, some defendants used the same lawyer after signing a waiver of conflict of interest. I represented several of these defendants. Since the transcripts and discovery were voluminous, it took months to digest all the relevant material.

After the dust settled, many Chinese felt their community had been wrongfully targeted. In its zeal to investigate the law office managers, the DA's Office had arguably entrapped the patients. Law enforcement ensnared people who were not pre-disposed to committing a crime and suggested the criminal activity. A prosecutor's role in society is to prevent crime, not manufacture it. Unfamiliarity with U.S. law and the criminal justice system caused the defendants extreme anxiety.

John DeLorean, famous for manufacturing a sleek, stainless steel sports car with gull-wing doors was arrested for drug trafficking, but acquitted in a famous 1982 case using the defense of entrapment. DeLorean, nicknamed the "Detroit Dream Merchant," left a $650,000 salary at General Motors to start his own automobile company. Stars such as Johnny Carson and Sammy Davis, Jr. invested millions into his venture.

Things soured in 1982 when DeLorean needed $17 million to save his business. An FBI informant, posing as a bank officer and another as a drug distributor made a deal with DeLorean. DeLorean's lawyer successfully argued that both the idea for the crime and the persuasion to perpetrate it came from government agents, not from DeLorean.

Most defendants in our insurance fraud case feared going to trial. They wanted to put this miserable episode behind them and get back to their lives. To be convicted of insurance fraud could result in a state prison sentence and deportation for non-citizens. These defendants were in a "Catch-22," an absurd predicament. If they wanted to be exonerated completely, they would have to go to trial. Then at trial, they would use the defense of entrapment. They might be acquitted, but there is always the risk of losing, especially with an entrapment defense. At trial, the defendant must admit the criminal conduct, then argue that, despite the fact he is guilty, he should be acquitted because he was entrapped. In such a case, jurors might not be so sympathetic, given the defendant's admission of his or her participation in the crime.

The defendant must prove that it is more likely than not that he or she was entrapped. A person is entrapped if a law enforcement agent engages in conduct, which would cause a normally law-abiding person to commit the crime. Examples of entrapment might include badgering, persuasion by flattery or coaxing, repeated and insistent requests, or an appeal to friendship or sympathy. Considered altogether, including the amiable, well-mannered nature of the undercover officer, many attorneys believed the DA's conduct would have made commission of the crime unusually attractive to an ordinarily law-abiding person. That included a suggestion that the offense would go undetected, so long as people remained quiet, as well as being an offer of extraordinary benefit, usually several thousand dollars.

After a year of court appearances, the parties arrived at various resolutions. Those defendants with serious criminal records and/or aggravated conduct in the case received felony convictions, some with jail or prison time. Some cases were dismissed outright. Others were settled as misdemeanors with minimal probation and no jail time. Most defendants, who admitted their culpability, would enter *nolo contendere* (no contest) pleas to misdemeanors, later to be dismissed prior to sentencing. Under California law, even if one pleads guilty or *nolo contendere*, choosing not to contest the charges, a conviction does not occur until a defendant is sentenced. These defendants had been through an ordeal, which introduced them to a shadowy aspect of American law enforcement. Sometimes, I tell my clients they have entered the twilight zone.

* * * * * * * *

The San Gabriel Valley stretches from Pasadena in the west to Pomona in the east, from Altadena in the north to Whittier in the south, forty cities in all, covering over two-hundred square miles housing almost two million people. The vast majority of the 500,000 Chinese residing in Los Angeles County live in the San Gabriel Valley, home to eight of the ten most Chinese populated cities in the US. Eighty years after the establishment of the San Gabriel Mission in 1771, Asian Americans – Chinese, Japanese, Filipinos, and South Asians – began to settle in the San Gabriel Valley. Now urbanized and a dynamic part of the Greater Los Angeles metropolitan area, this valley began as an agricultural community. The *padres* of the San Gabriel Mission cultivated limes, pomegranates, peaches, pears, figs and apples.

Over time, acres of grape vines and orange groves arose from the valley's fertile soils. The new settlers worked in citrus and grape fields. To our present day benefit, they laid the foundations of a basic infrastructure. In 1882, the Chinese Exclusion Act prohibited further immigration which left Chinese Americans isolated, as they were now barred from bringing their families to the United States. In 1900, the region that became the City of San Gabriel in 1913, was a Western village with its own Chinatown. Traveling from house to house in one-horse wagons, Chinese vegetable salesmen offered their produce for sale. Many Chinese worked on farms, picking citrus and vegetables, caring for the land. Chinese cooks were favored by the area's well to do.

It wasn't until 1965 and President Johnson's landmark Immigration Act, signed at the base of the Statue of Liberty, that a new surge of Chinese would come to America and the San Gabriel Valley. The number of first-generation immigrants living in the US quadrupled from slightly less than ten million in 1970 to approximately forty million in 2012. The San Gabriel Valley's rapidly increasing Chinese population, with its distinctive business districts, was exemplified by the City of Monterey Park, called "Little Taipei" in the 1970s and 1980s. Realtors during this era marketed Monterey Park to affluent potential immigrants back in Taiwan as the "Chinese Beverly Hills." Monterey Park was the pioneering city for wealthy Chinese, and was the model for the term "ethnoburb," a suburban residential and business area of a particular ethnic minority population, coined in 1997 by Dr. Wei Li, professor of Asian Pacific Studies at Arizona State University. The City of Monterey Park boasts the highest percentage of Chinese residents of any municipality in the US, but is no longer preferred by wealthy Chinese immigrants who now purchase their homes in San Marino, Arcadia, Walnut and Diamond Bar.

The San Gabriel Valley Chinese community flourishes. Billboards and signs in bold Mandarin characters advertise Chinese-owned businesses. Neighborhoods are filled with Chinese supermarkets, doctors of traditional oriental medicine, acupuncture, acupressure, and reflexology. Martial arts and Chinese ballet classes are offered at many neighborhood strip malls. There are Feng-shui consultants; Chinese opera and holiday festivals, dragon parades, moon cakes, and red envelopes; Tai Chi in municipal parks and Tiger Moms in the PTA. Rich business, social, and cultural cords between the San Gabriel Valley and Asia generate optimism and promise that resonate around the globe.

The dream of a comfortable life in the San Gabriel Valley lured David Hao to move from his home in Taipei, Taiwan to an apartment in Monterey Park. Mr. Hao, a melancholic, elderly Chinese man, had spent his entire savings on his only asset, a small motel located on a busy street near the USC campus, south of downtown Los Angeles. On a scorching summer afternoon, the Los Angeles Police Department stationed a female undercover officer in front of the motel. Dressed in an eye-catching red miniskirt, her job was to solicit men to join her in a room for sex at Mr. Hao's motel. She succeeded in ensnaring two customers, several hours apart. Mr. Hao employed a college-age worker to man the registration desk. The undercover officer and customer would register in the motel lobby, renting a room for two hours. They would then walk to and enter the motel room, where a second officer would arrest the customer. It is a municipal code violation to rent rooms for only a few hours and Mr. Hao was cited. Mr. Hao hired me and I fought the citation in court. Ultimately the charge was dropped and that was the end of it. Or so we thought.

Several months later, Mr. Hao received a notice from the City of Los Angeles Zoning Department declaring his motel a nuisance, and the city's intent to seize the property. Mr. Hao had devoted his life to this motel and now the city was going to take it from him. He hired me again. I obtained copies of the two prostitution arrest reports used as the basis for the nuisance allegation. I took statements from Mr. Hao's friends and business acquaintances who declared him a man of good character. I also talked to local homeless people who were regularly offered rooms when the motel was not fully occupied. I learned through my investigation that a large church directly across the street coveted Mr. Hao's land to build an addition. Pressure had been put on the city to have Mr. Hao's property declared a nuisance so the church could purchase the land at below market value. I filed a brief with the City of Los Angeles Zoning Department detailing Mr. Hao's history and arguing that his motel was not a nuisance, but rather a benefit to the neighborhood. He helped homeless families, paid his taxes and was a considerate neighbor. In the brief, I included character references and statements from the homeless people Mr. Hao had helped.

I appeared at the public hearing with Mr. Hao. There was a huge crowd abuzz with onlookers. When I prepared the paperwork, I alleged the secret motivation for this proceeding was to assist the church in obtaining Mr. Hao's property. Before the hearing, I believed I had no way of proving this motivation, so I expected the hearing officer to disregard this unproven allegation. At the hearing, the large crowd was composed of many church congregants. They were there to tell the city of the church's plans and need for the property. When I realized this, I called the most vocal of the attendees to testify. They were happy to tell the Hearing Officer of the church's desire for the property. The undercover officer and her partner also testified. I cross-examined the attractive fake prostitute based on the arrest reports. I asked, "It was you who set up these crimes, wasn't it? It was you who chose this location? It was you who brought the sex customers to this motel? It was you who directed the customers to park in the motel parking lot?" At the end of the hearing, I argued, "How outrageous this hearing, how unfair these accusations! The city set up the crime, chose the location and then decided to take the property because of the crimes occurring at the location, crimes the city brought to the motel." The Hearing Officer, although a politician by nature, saw through the charade and simply ordered Mr. Hao to hang "No Prostitution" signs at the motel. He then dismissed the accusation, upsetting the church congregation, but doing the right thing. Hallelujah.

* * * * * * * *

Chapter II

Launching My Career
The District Attorney's Office

The initial mystery that attends any journey is how did the
traveler reach his starting point in the first place.
— Louise Bogan

On June 13, 1984, standing before a Los Angeles County
Superior Court Judge, I solemnly swore to uphold the
Constitutions of the United States of America and the State
of California. Attorneys call this the "swearing-in" ceremony,
after which the applicant is officially licensed to practice law.
Several months later, I took a similar oath in the law offices
of the Los Angeles County District Attorney. The new DA,
Ira Reiner, standing directly in front of me, elevated his right
hand, ordered me to raise mine, and swore me in. This ceremony
was documented with a photograph. Aware of the illustrious
and dramatic history of the DA's office, including its famous
prosecutions of Charles Manson and Sirhan Sirhan, I proudly

accepted my badge and a temporary assignment at Eastlake Juvenile Court. After four months of arraigning, prosecuting, negotiating and adjudicating juvenile cases, I transferred to a permanent assignment at West Covina Municipal Court.

* * * * * * * *

John Baumann, the Deputy DA in Charge (DIC) assigned me as a Calendar Deputy to Division 5, Judge Alex Lozano's court. Baumann, well regarded for his successful jury trial record, now as an administrator took pride in training young deputies to be competent trial lawyers. My first day in Division 5 was a smoggy Wednesday, April 1985. Judge Lozano was a soft-spoken heavyset man with a round face, who often mumbled his words. I entered the courtroom with a stack of fifty files. Most were arraignments and pretrial hearings. About a dozen were jury trials. There were misdemeanor cases involving drunk-driving, shoplifting, battery, trespassing and prostitution. In addition, there were several felonies (assault with a deadly weapon, burglary, narcotics) set for preliminary hearing. A preliminary hearing is an evidentiary hearing where witnesses are called to testify against a defendant. The prosecutor has the obligation of establishing a reasonable suspicion that a crime was committed and that the defendant is responsible. The standard of proof at this level is very modest. "Any evidence, however slight" is sufficient probable cause for the court to hold a defendant to answer for the crime. At a preliminary hearing, the judge may choose one of three rulings. He can dismiss the case for lack of proof; he can hold the defendant to answer to the charges; or he can reduce a felony charge to a misdemeanor if the statute allows.

West Covina Court had a reputation of being a bit odd. I learned that on day one. A defendant on a petty case was called before the court. He was Spanish-speaking only and had a right to an interpreter. When his name was called, he stepped forward and said, "Español." While West Covina had several Spanish interpreters, none were in the courtroom. Judge Lozano looked at his court reporter, Manuel Velasquez, and then shot a quick glance at me. The judge conducted the entire proceeding in Spanish with Velasquez typing the conversation in English. I understood nothing. The man thanked the court and left. I thought, "What was that?" but said nothing. It was my first day and I was not about to make waves. Later that afternoon in Baumann's office, I described the event. I reviewed the court file prior to entering his office, and now understood the Spanish speaker was only seeking an extension to pay a fine. I interrupted Baumann talking to Wayne Miller, a senior Deputy DA and member of the DA's Hardcore Gang Unit. Baumann was unconcerned with the Spanish-speaking case. Several years later, both Baumann and Miller were appointed judges to the Superior Court by Governor George Deukmejian. Late Friday afternoon, two days after I started, Judge Lozano asked me to do him a favor. Pointing to the Penal Code, he told me, "Take that sacred book home and study it carefully over the weekend."

By the end of my assignment in West Covina, I had frequently appeared before all eight of the courthouse judges, handled thousands of cases including scores of preliminary hearings and about thirty misdemeanor jury trials. The majority of the misdemeanors I tried were drunk-driving cases. Other trials included trespassing, vandalism, marijuana and narcotics, petty theft, reckless driving, joy riding, assault and misdemeanor manslaughter. Misdemeanor manslaughter is defined as the commission of an act without gross negligence, not amounting to a felony, which results in the killing of a human being. Any traffic infraction resulting in death could be charged as misdemeanor manslaughter, punishable by up to one year in the county jail.

I lived on Beachwood Drive in the Hollywood Hills, a thirty-minute drive to the courthouse. West Covina is a small middle-class community east of Los Angeles. In the two years I was assigned to this court, I spent time learning the neighborhood, eating at ethnic restaurants, strolling in the mall and meeting my colleagues at local watering holes. One day, while shopping at a West Covina store, I ran into a man I knew, but could not remember how. He had the same recognizing yet quizzical look on his face. We both smiled and began talking, wondering how we knew each other. It hit us both at the same awkward moment: I had prosecuted him. We both stopped smiling. I left in a hurry.

As I was handling many of the cases filed by the local police department, I befriended some of the local police detectives. A triple murder occurred in West Covina, and I was asked by a homicide detective to review a search warrant and accompany the detectives to the crime scene. Detectives had previously been to the scene and secured it, but they sought a warrant for a detailed search of the premises including cabinets, drawers and locked containers. Three dead bodies were sprawled on the ground like discarded mannequins. They looked unreal. Wearing latex gloves, the coroner's investigator touched every part of the corpses looking for bullet holes. It was an out-of-body experience for me. From a viewpoint above the room, I saw myself standing below.

At West Covina, I was trying misdemeanor cases and doing felony preliminary hearings. It is every young Deputy DA's desire to try felony cases, which gets a young Deputy noticed at the time of promotion. West Covina Area Court feeds Pomona Branch Court its felonies. I made it clear to the Head Deputy in Pomona that Deputy Perliss wanted a felony trial. One day I received a call that a felony burglary trial was waiting for me. I packed my briefcase and drove to Pomona Court. Reading through the file, I recognized the weak nature of the evidence. Nobody in the Pomona Branch DA's Office would try this case. After interviewing the witnesses, I realized the case was actually worse than it appeared on paper. I discussed the problems with the Head Deputy. He asked that I present the evidence and let the jury decide. I did. In closing argument, in an effort to protect the reputation of the DA's office as fair, I did not argue. I merely thanked the jurors for sacrificing their time to participate in this trial. The defense attorney retorted, "You just heard the prosecutor not ask you to find the defendant guilty." The members of the jury looked at me. I looked back at them. Thereafter, the jury was instructed. They deliberated for five minutes, finding the defendant not guilty.

After almost two years in West Covina, I was anxious for a transfer to felony trials, specifically Central Trials at the Criminal Courts Building in downtown Los Angeles, a court where I had many friends. I asked John Baumann to help me transfer. He called Alex Burke, the DA in charge of transfers, and recommended me. Burke would need to think about it, investigate me, talk to others and then make the decision. Immediately after John's phone call, I dispatched two senior DA friends into Burke's office. They told Burke they heard I was being transferred to Central Trials and that I would be a great addition. This tactic succeeded. Two weeks later, I started work at Central Trials.

When I later told my father, he said, "Burke didn't have a chance." Dad always gets to the heart of the matter. When I was sixteen, I rear-ended a car and was ticketed for an infraction. I was summoned before the Juvenile Traffic Court. The referee asked my father, "How's your son doing at home and school?" Dad told him I was doing well in school and at home, but unfortunately my batting average on the baseball team was suffering. They both laughed and I was excused.

* * * * * * * *

I was now assigned to CT 13 (Central Felony Trials, 13th Floor Courts). My supervisor was William Katz, my office mate Sarah Levine. Sarah and I were assigned as trial deputies for Department 124, Judge Wallace Worthington. Judge Worthington was a big man with white hair and a face so crimson he was known as Red Worthington. By the time I met him, he was elderly and had been a judge many years. Some decades earlier as an officer of the Los Angeles Police Department, he had been a member of the famous "Hat Squad," so called because of their fedoras and sharp tailor-made, single-breasted suits. *The Los Angeles Times* wrote about the four LAPD Robbery Division members of the 1950s and 1960s. "They were tough with criminals but very compassionate people, respected in the underworld." In the 1996 movie, *Mulholland Falls*, Nick Nolte played a member of the "Hat Squad." In a ridiculously dramatic scene, a bashed-up mafia kingpin about to get thrown off a cliff protests, "You can't do this in America." Nolte wryly quips: "This ain't America, Jack. This is L.A." After his time in the police department, Worthington became a Court Commissioner, then Municipal Court Judge, finally Superior Court Judge.

Katz handed me my first murder case, a shooting that occurred in Leimert Park in Los Angeles near the University of Southern California. Defendants Ben Fugit and Dennis Dugan were charged with first-degree murder. Murder is the unlawful killing of a human being, with malice aforethought. First-degree murder occurs when a defendant deliberates or premeditates the killing. Defendant Fugit was accused of shooting the victim, and Defendant Dugan was thought to have aided Fugit in the act. California law does not distinguish between the principal and the aider and abettor of a crime. A common example of this is a bank robbery in the old West. Three outlaws ride up to a bank. Two of the men rob the bank killing a teller. One stays outside holding the horses and acting as lookout. The bandit outside is not only equally guilty of the robbery, but also guilty of murder under the felony murder rule.

The photographs of the victim were grotesque. The entrance wound in the forehead was a small hole; the exit wound spread across most of the side of the victim's head. The two defendants had been on a mission to kill a man who had earlier attacked Fugit's brother. They drove around much of the night looking for their target, who had long since left the scene. Instead, they vented their revenge on an innocent bystander. Each defendant was represented by counsel. Fugit's attorney was Anton Madrid, in his late 60s, renowned in Hollywood circles, having represented many famous actors. Madrid was smooth as silk. While picking the jury, he memorized all of the jurors' names and one interesting aspect of their answers. In a folksy and personable voice and without notes, he would address them by name and talk to them about an answer they had given to the judge hours earlier. When I mentioned how impressive his *voir dire* skills were, he told me, "It is not difficult, Sandy, just pay attention, practice, try it in your next trial." Despite Madrid's courtroom skills, both defendants were convicted of first-degree murder.

It wasn't as easy as Madrid suggested, and in my next murder trial I made a complete fool of myself. During *voir dire*, I had impressively remembered eleven juror names. The twelfth was a middle-aged African American whose surname was Brown. To my profound embarrassment, I addressed him as "Mr. Black." This trial involved a drive-by shooting. The defendant maneuvered his truck alongside the target vehicle. The victim, a passenger, was completely unaware of what was about to happen. The assailant and sole occupant of the truck aimed a handgun at the victim's head and pulled the trigger, killing him instantly. As the driver of the victim's car watched in horror, he recognized the assailant who was now aiming the pistol at him. Quickly flooring the gas pedal, the driver sped away. This witness's testimony was the only direct evidence against the accused. His identification was bolstered by the fact that he knew the defendant. The jury returned a verdict of second-degree murder.

In addition to murder trials, I tried other felonies, some very serious. There were trials with charges of robbery, narcotics, receiving stolen property, assault with a deadly weapon and grand theft. There was a case where a stranger dressed in black was found late at night in a backyard of a home that had just been burglarized. The defense that the suspect "just happened to be there" was silly. I highlighted the absurdity of the defense by telling the jury a story in my closing argument. "A twenty-five year bank employee with a perfect attendance record, let's call him Bill, developed a migraine headache at work. He had never taken a sick day before. On this day, his head hurt so badly he could hardly think. He tried to remain at work but by two o'clock, he couldn't take it anymore and asked his boss for the rest of the day off. He was having a horrible day. If his head hadn't hurt so much, he would have noticed his best friend's car parked in front of his home. Bill drove into his garage and walked in the house. Because his head was throbbing, he didn't think anything of it when he saw his wife at the bedroom door dressed in lingerie and sipping a glass of champagne. He did not stop to hug her. He just wanted to get to bed. He did not realize his bed was unmade. He went to the closet and took off his suit. Removing his tie, he noticed his friend, Al, hiding behind a row of hanging garments. 'Al,' he said, 'what are you doing here?'

'Well, Bill, everybody's gotta be somewhere.' And that, Ladies and Gentlemen, is what this defendant wants you to believe."

* * * * * * * *

Flamboyant Oscar Levy was famous in the criminal courts. He practiced for years and knew everybody. At an extravagant outdoor cocktail party, he brazenly trotted in on a white horse. My first case against Oscar was a narcotics case; he sent an associate to stand in for him to postpone the trial. Oscar could not be present on the day set for the court trial. The man he sent was an older, tired lawyer. The lawyer defended the case to the best of his ability. Intimidated each time the judge spoke, he nervously made objections, tentatively questioning the witness. The defendant spent a lot of money for Oscar Levy. Oscar was in another court defending a different client when this case was called. A criminal lawyer cannot be two places at the same time. The judge would not postpone the matter, forcing the worn out lawyer to complete the trial. Of course, the defendant was unhappy that he was being defended by a man he did not know and did not seem to be doing a particularly good job. The defendant was charged with possession of crack cocaine with intent to sell.

The defendant had earlier agreed to waive his right to a jury trial, allowing the judge to decide the issue of guilt. I put the prosecution witness on the stand. The officer who had removed the drugs from the defendant's pocket testified how the drugs were cut, kept in distinct portions, and found with several hundred dollars. This evidence suggested the defendant possessed the drugs for purposes of sale. The defense attorney raised next to no defense at all. The judge found the defendant guilty of possession for purposes of sale.

Soon after, Oscar appeared and argued the lawyer he sent was not qualified to conduct the trial and had only been directed to postpone it until Oscar could be present. Of course, this argument had been made earlier by the substitute attorney. Having seen the elderly lawyer's performance, perhaps the judge felt trying the case with him was a mistake. The judge set aside the conviction and decided to re-try the case. He ordered me to recall the witness. The testimony was almost identical. The difference was Oscar Levy. In an aggressive tone, Oscar took a tough stance against the witness, punching and jabbing, although only using his voice. Oscar's only argument was that his client did not possess the drugs for sale. There were plenty of drugs found in the defendant's possession, cut into small pieces, all the better to sell. But Oscar argued the narcotics could have been possessed for personal use. The fact that the drugs were cut and sealed in different packaging did not mean they were for sale. In stark contrast to his earlier ruling, the judge, who permitted this unusual re-trial, agreed with Oscar that the drugs might not have been possessed for sale. Perhaps the drugs were kept for personal use only. The judge found the defendant guilty of possession and dismissed the "possession for sale" count. Oscar's client received a modest county jail sentence.

* * * * * * * *

*Change is the law of life and those who look only to the past or
present are certain to miss the future.*
– John F. Kennedy

Dr. Solomon Rose, my childhood friend, has come a long way since our boyhood days. He lives in the Hollywood Hills and has many friends and patients among the Hollywood elite. One of his friends, Jack Reilly, owned an art gallery in Beverly Hills. Solomon and I would occasionally attend openings at the gallery and stay for dinner. At one such dinner, Jack introduced me to the guests as Deputy DA Sandy Perliss. A fascinating mix of people were drinking fine wines, savoring gourmet foods, enjoying contemporary art and stimulating conversation. Feeling a sense of distance, I kept wondering how many of them I would later prosecute for DUI. Maybe they were thinking the same way. I realized then that I had become too one-dimensional, lacking depth and balance, unable to enjoy a conversation with an artist and incapable of seeing a rich palette of colors. Instead, I perceived only right and wrong, black and white, and a few shades of gray. This event triggered a major change in my life. I was no longer comfortable as a Deputy District Attorney and wanted freedom from this identity.

I prosecuted over a thousand cases and was doing well in the office, on track for early promotion. However, as a government lawyer, I was not earning enough money and was tired of William telling me how to try cases. I wanted to be my own boss, controlling my own destiny. The following Monday, I drafted a letter to my supervisor thanking him and the DA's Office for the remarkable experience. I stated that I was resigning effective two weeks from the date of the letter.

That ended my years as a prosecutor. When Judge Worthington heard, he called me into his chambers. "Perliss, have you done the math? Do you know how much money you need to keep a private office going?"

Despite the challenges, I was ready to enter private practice.

Chapter III

Into the Fire: Murder, Robbery & Kidnapping

The only real lawyers are trial lawyers,
and trial lawyers try cases to juries.
— Clarence Darrow

Criminal defense lawyers are ethically obligated to vigorously defend their clients, in spite of the horrible crimes the clients are accused of committing. I have been to gatherings where people ask what I do for a living. I tell them I am a criminal defense lawyer. Often I hear, "How can you do that? That's immoral." I usually answer by citing the Fifth Amendment of the Constitution, which gives everyone the right to an attorney. The State is represented by a zealous advocate and since the criminal justice system is adversarial, a defendant has the same right. The criminal justice system presumes a confrontation between evenly trained and skilled opponents and expects such encounter will result in a fair and just outcome. When the individual is not so represented, the adversarial system fails. Then, I tell the self-righteous critic, "God forbid you get into serious trouble. I am the first person you will call."

Criminal defense lawyers are not bad people. They are often the individual's last stand against an aggressive prosecution. In this law and order society, occasionally otherwise law-abiding people are prosecuted where the behavior or alleged crime does not necessarily merit the severe punishment. For serious criminal charges, you hope the lawyer is experienced, which means he or she has represented many defendants. Clarence Darrow wrote: "You can only protect your liberties in this world by protecting the other man's freedom."

There are two ways to make a living as a criminal defense lawyer. The most obvious is to hang a shingle and take in business. This requires patience. While building one's private practice, criminal lawyers can also accept court-appointed cases. After I left the District Attorney's Office, I hung that proverbial shingle and joined the Los Angeles County Bar Association's Indigent Criminal Defense Panel which assigned me court appointed cases. One such case was *The People of the State of California vs. Thomas Worthy.* My client, an old man, was charged with committing a strong-armed robbery. He and three others were accused of forcibly taking money, documents and a wallet from an unsuspecting victim who unluckily happened to walk past the assailants. Because of the volume of street crime, the police department stationed patrol officers on the second floor of a Skid Row hotel to observe the pedestrians below. The officers witnessed the robbery and radioed back that four men, between the ages of twenty-five and thirty, wearing long trench coats, had robbed a victim and run off. The officers pursued the suspects and apprehended all four. When caught, the suspects were wearing long trench coats. In the possession of one of the suspects, the police found the victim's name typed on a stolen letter. I was appointed to represent one of these defendants, Thomas Worthy. Mr. Worthy had a worn, deeply wrinkled face.

When I met Mr. Worthy, we had a lengthy discussion about his background and the facts leading to his arrest. He understood the proceedings, my role, and answered my questions appropriately. But he was not all there. He had been homeless for many years. He showed me a trick. He could multiply any number by nine, even numbers in the thousands and immediately know the answer. He wore an ankle-length trench coat which he used as a blanket to keep him warm at night. The case resulted in a jury trial before my old friend, Judge Wallace Worthington. The DA gave an opening statement, telling the jury the police witnessed a strong-armed robbery. The officers observed four assailants grab the victim, beat him and take his property. The DA continued, "The officers will identify the four defendants as being the assailants." In his opening, the DA did not mention the officers' initial description of the suspects. Opening statements are designed to outline to the jury what the attorney believes the evidence will show. An attorney is not supposed to use opening statements to argue his or her case. He or she is only permitted to summarize the case and the evidence. Sometimes, attorneys will sneak in a little argument. When this happens, often the lawyer will be scolded by the judge. Occasionally, the lawyer might get away with it.

In my opening statement, I told the jury, "Youth is a gift of nature, age a work of art." Then I sat down. A bemused Judge Worthington raised his eyebrows at me. The DA called his witnesses, the victim and the officers. The victim could not (or would not) identify any of the defendants. The officers had no trouble identifying all four. I cross-examined each officer about the description of the assailants written in the police report. I asked, "Did you review the police report? Did you find any errors in the report? Did you request any changes in the report? Isn't it true that the four assailants were described as between the ages of twenty-five and thirty? As you look at Mr. Worthy today, does he look as if he is in his twenties or thirties?" Usually, in closing argument, lawyers emphasize how the prosecution has the burden of proof beyond a reasonable doubt and that in this case, the prosecution has failed. Instead, I simply reminded the jury that youth is a gift of nature, age a work of art. The judge smiled. The jury returned a verdict of not guilty. That was the last time I saw Thomas Worthy.

Over a decade later, I received a phone call from the Los Angeles County Coroner's Office that a homeless man's body was discovered in a Skid Row alley. His identification and my crumpled old business card were found in his pocket. The coroner's investigator asked if I knew the decedent, a Mr. Thomas Worthy, and if I had any information about his next of kin.

This was the second time the coroner's office contacted me with next of kin questions. The other time involved an elderly black man named Jackie Simpkins. Mr. Simpkins walked into my 7th Street downtown Los Angeles office without an appointment and inquired if he could meet with the lawyer. My secretary asked if I would see him, then brought him in. He was a gentle, soft-spoken, thin man dressed in a navy blue suit and burgundy tie. He showed me his phone bill and asked if I could help him because the phone company was charging an extra $4.95 per month. I reviewed the bill and called the phone company, telling them my client did not ask for this service and to delete the charge. They were happy to comply. I handed back Mr. Simpkins' phone bill and said, "Success." He was pleased, took out his wallet and asked how much he owed me. I told him it was on the house, but to keep my business card. We argued. Finally, I told him it was only two minutes of my time and I would not take his money. Later I was sorry to learn he gave my secretary $40 on his way out. It was the last I heard about Mr. Simpkins until the coroner's office called.

* * * * * * * *

I was hired by the family of Tyrone Madlock to represent Tyrone against a murder charge in the Criminal Courts Building, downtown Los Angeles. Tyrone was an OG (Original Gangster), known as T Dog. One Saturday night, Tyrone threw a party for his neighborhood friends. Many people attended. One neighbor had been drinking earlier and appeared at the party without a shirt. Intoxicated, he spent much of the time hassling the guests. Tyrone angrily insisted the man leave and forced him out the door. As Tyrone pushed him out, he did something unusual. He kissed the man's cheek.

Later that evening, about a mile away, a confrontation occurred between the shirtless man and an assailant. The assailant drew a handgun and shot three bullets into the shirtless torso. Before the shooting, the victim yelled, "Dawg, why you do this to me?" A one-eyed homeless man heard the yell and saw the shooting with his one good eye, although he could not identify anyone. The shooting happened at an intersection across from a hamburger stand. The owner of the hamburger stand was working that evening. It was a little too far away to make an identification, but he did see the shooting.

An investigation ensued. The police heard the victim had been at the party earlier and forcibly removed by Tyrone.

They learned the strange fact that Tyrone had kissed the man's cheek. Detectives associated that kiss with a mafia-style death kiss. They also knew Tyrone's gang name, T Dog. Tyrone was charged with first-degree murder, punishable by twenty-five years to life in prison. With his criminal record, Tyrone would never get out.

I went to see the hamburger stand owner and bought a burger. He talked to me about his business and what he observed on the night of the murder. I asked if the police report was accurate regarding his inability to see the face of the assailant. He said that was true, yet he could tell the general size of the man. He said the man was bigger and taller than me, by at least two inches, and that the police did not ask for a general description. They only wanted to know if he could identify the shooter. Tyrone was at least an inch shorter than me.

I continued to look for witnesses and found the one-eyed man with the shopping cart. My investigator and I talked to him. Surprising us with a slight but significant modification in his recollection, he told us he heard the victim say, "Lawd, why you do this to me?" Since this would be used as impeachment, challenging witness credibility, I was not required to share with the DA this nuanced change.

The DA had a bright future. He was confident and absolutely certain my client was guilty. He tried his best to obtain a conviction. But the cards were stacked against him. On the first morning of scheduled testimony, I asked which witness he would call. He had several witnesses present and ready to testify. "Why don't you call that businessman first?" I was pointing to the hamburger stand owner. "Let him get back to running his business." The DA agreed it was a good idea. From the DA's perspective, starting the case with a handsome, hardworking businessman was ideal to set the scene and atmosphere of the shooting. The DA started with questions about the location, the lighting and the distance. Then, he brought out a diagram and inquired of the witness where on the diagram the shooting took place, where this witness was at the time and the positioning of the streetlights. The DA presented the photographs and had the witness retell the story using the photographs. This is a common strategy we learned in DA training. By the time you are done with direct examination of the witness, you have succeeded in having the witness tell the story three times. Finally, the DA proudly told the judge he had no further questions of this witness. The judge looked at me, "Cross- examination, Mr. Perliss."

I asked the witness if he was able to see the shooter's face. He could not. I asked if he could describe him. "Yes, he was about 6 feet tall with a medium build."

I stood erect and told the witness I was 5'9". "Was he taller than me?"

"Yes," he said, "by a couple of inches."

I walked over to my client and stood next to him. "Your Honor, with the Court's permission, may Mr. Madlock stand." Madlock stood, two inches shorter than me. "Directing your attention to the man standing next to me, is this the height and general body shape of the shooter?"

"No," said the DA's ideal first witness.

"Thank you, Sir, I have no further questions." The DA lost the case with his first witness.

The next witness, the one-eyed homeless man, took the stand. He was asked about the shooting and responded as well as he could remember. When asked what he heard the victim yell just before being shot, he said the man howled, "Lawd, why you do this to me?"

The DA was taken by surprise. "Didn't you previously assert the man said, 'Dawg, why you do this to me?'?"

The witness responded, "Maybe the man said Dawg, but I really think I heard Lawd." The DA had a very bad day. After two weeks in trial, the jury acquitted Mr. Madlock.

* * * * * * * *

My next jury trial, the *United States of America vs. Sophia Divac*, was in Northern California, referred by Mel Goldfarb, an old law school classmate, now working at an international law firm in San Francisco. Born and raised in Serbia and brought to America at sixteen by parents seeking a safe environment, Sophia was now charged with conspiracy to commit robbery. She was a teller supervisor at the San Francisco branch of a public employee credit union. Her childhood friend, Viktor Pesa, from the same hometown in Serbia, and a former credit union teller, would often visit Sophia at work. One day a tall Caucasian man, Andrew Lekovic, entered the bank, walked to a teller window and aimed a handgun at Sophia, who at that very moment was pushing a cart full of cash to the vault. The gun stayed aimed at Sophia while Lekovic waited for her to load the money into a bag. Lekovic exited the bank and ran several blocks to an awaiting car. Several credit union employees, including Sophia, followed the assailant out of the credit union. The car sped off and a high-speed chase and shootout ensued with the local police eventually arresting Lekovic and the getaway driver. Lekovic, also of Serbian descent, was shot and taken to the jail ward of the hospital. The driver, unharmed, was Sophia's good friend, Viktor, the one who had visited her so often at the credit union.

Lekovic had a criminal record spanning thirty years, including a previous bank robbery and numerous violent crimes.

Because of his record and the gravity of the current charges, he was likely to spend much of the rest of his life in federal prison. His only chance was to cooperate with the government against his alleged co-conspirators. Pleading guilty at the pretrial stage, Lekovic gave a complete statement about how he, Viktor and Sophia had planned the robbery, the other two providing the gun. According to him, Sophia had divulged the exact time she would be moving the cart toward the vault.

I was hired to represent Sophia in court. I filed a motion to sever the case and separate Sophia from the other defendant, Viktor, who, minimizing his own culpability, insisted he would testify Sophia was the mastermind. That motion was denied. I prepared for trial, spending many hours with Sophia going over the evidence and interviewing Sophia's colleagues who were present during the robbery.

In my opening statement, I told the jury my client was the victim of a friend who used his relationship as a pretext to study the credit union's procedures. I suggested throughout the case that Sophia was set up by the other two, Viktor and Lekovic. Since we feared having to defend against the informant, Lekovic, and the potential testimony of the former friend, Viktor, it was every person for herself.

The trial proceeded with credit union employee witnesses who were present at the time of the robbery. One witness, who set the scene of the robbery on direct examination, conceded under cross-examination that Sophia was the individual who pressed the emergency button. Another colleague testified Sophia was a loyal employee. A supervisor confirmed that Sophia had keys to the credit union. Later, I argued that since she had keys, she would not need to stage a robbery, that she could just take the money after hours. The actual robber took the stand and testified about meetings he had with Viktor and Sophia to plan the robbery. Lekovic testified about how the other two planned it, told him when to arrive and provided him with the gun. I impeached him with crimes he had committed. There were at least fifteen of them. We talked about his convictions, including robberies, burglaries and aggravated assaults. I learned from cross-examination he had testified in earlier cases against other co-defendants. I suggested he learned how to commit crimes and then weasel his way out of punishment by lying about other people. I submitted that since he would spend most of the rest of his life in prison, he had no choice but to help the prosecution at any cost, even if it meant fabricating a story about an innocent person.

I decided the defense was strong enough that Sophia need not testify. Viktor, the co-defendant, also chose not to testify. After witness examinations, it was time for closing argument. The Assistant U.S. Attorney began, "Ladies and Gentlemen, this is a case about greed," and then proceeded to tell the jury about "the greed of the defendants."

When he finished, it was my turn. I said, "Ladies and Gentlemen, the prosecutor is correct, this *is* a case about greed. It is about the greed of Andrew Lekovic who viciously stole money at gunpoint, engaged in a shootout to avoid apprehension, and in desperation, bore false witness against an innocent person." Then I used Lekovic's background to argue the only way he could save his freedom was to give the government something they did not already have, the phantom bank insider. The jury found Sophia not guilty.

* * * * * * *

The defendant's right to a fair trial is supreme. Sending an innocent person to prison is a grave moral failure, more so than acquitting a guilty person. A lawyer must suspend his or her judgment of the client who allegedly commits an egregious crime. There is no requirement however, that deep inside, the attorney believe the client's story. Innocent or not, an attorney's duty is to hold the state to its obligation of proving guilt beyond a reasonable doubt, as illustrated in the following.

Griffith Park is a wonder of nature: oaks, walnuts, sycamores, dense chaparral, and holly berry, from which Hollywood is named. It is a beautiful mountainside habitat of deer, coyote, gray fox, lizards, purple finch, red-breasted bluebirds; a setting for hiking, tennis, golf and horseback riding. There is an observatory and planetarium where families explore the sky and stars together.

A large mountainous expanse, however, can have its problems: many hidden, secluded places, where from time to time hikers find discarded, lifeless bodies. In the spring of 1992, a small woman's body was discovered bound, wrapped in a blanket cinched by a belt, inside a garbage bag, dropped thirty-five feet down an embankment. The body was hog-tied, hands behind back, legs to hands. A rag had been stuffed in the mouth, an electric cord twisted around the neck. No identification was found. It would take six weeks for the police to identify the body.

Fingerprints matching Xavier Moore, a petty criminal, were discovered on the Hefty garbage bag. Detectives investigated the victim's background and located witnesses. According to those witnesses, Moore worked for Tony Rivers, a drug dealing, violent, nasty thug. The victim also worked for Rivers. Rivers would entrust rock cocaine to the victim to sell. After a sale was made, she would return and give Rivers the cash. Often she would come back short a rock or missing money. She was stealing. Her last transaction resulted in missing dope. Rivers had enough. He and Moore stripped, hog-tied and placed her in a water-filled bathtub. They tortured her to death, put the corpse in a Hefty bag and concealed it in a car where it was driven to a remote area in Griffith Park.

Rivers and Moore were arrested. I was appointed to represent Moore. The case lingered at the pre-trial stage for over a year. Motions were filed and argued, evidence collected and analyzed, witnesses located and interviewed, and eventually the trial was set. It was a particularly horrible and gruesome crime. When the trial started, neither co-counsel nor I had any idea of a defense. We had extremely unsympathetic clients with a mountain of evidence against us.

All parties agreed to try the case in Night Court. In those days, I was single, no wife and children waiting for me at home. On the clock, billing for my time, I did not mind the extra hours. The five-month trial in Night Court would be in session from 3 p.m. to 9 p.m. I was young and energetic, able to handle my daytime caseload, my court appearances in the morning, evidentiary hearings in the afternoon and trial at night.

The murder case dragged on, night after night, witness after witness. Attorney Robert Perry, when making a summation in the John DeLorean trial, said, "For a plot hatched in hell, don't expect angels for witnesses." The absence of angels was especially true in this case. The witnesses were drug dealers, users, prostitutes and street criminals. These witnesses testified the victim was stealing from Rivers. Moore and Rivers killed her for it.

At the end of the trial, I argued that, given their extensive criminal records, the witnesses were not credible. I also argued the insufficiency of evidence of pre-meditation. So, if the jury found Moore guilty of murder, it would be murder in the second degree. I did not have a lot to work with, except the character of the DA's witnesses. The jury could not reach a verdict. The DA and the judge were frustrated. The judge declared a mistrial, which I considered a small victory, although I knew in the long run, my client would be convicted. The case was returned to the master calendar court. Four months later, the case was set for trial in a different courtroom. This time, it went to a harsh judge, committed to concluding the trial within two months. The DA cleaned up her witnesses' testimony.

The new judge spent most of the time angry. He obviously had issues other than the ones in this case. He had read through the transcript of the first trial and predetermined the outcome. He had an agenda. He didn't like me, my energy, my fight. Later an elderly lawyer told me the Judge was sometimes hardest on young lawyers. He made life unbearable during the re-trial, impossible to get any defense across to the jury. This is not so unusual. There is a tactic when an attorney is before such an intemperate judge. The goal is to ensure the jury sees the judge's bias. The jury, after a while, would get the impression the judge was being heavy-handed with the defense. The more hostile, the better. I did not have a strong argument in this case, but if the jury watched me constantly beaten up by the judge, I would concentrate in final argument on the defendant's right to a fair trial. In argument, I did not say anything specific about this judge. I argued about due process and equal protection under the law. The DA had a much stronger case this time around. The issue of the constitutional right to a fair trial was all I had. The jury did not care. Rivers and Moore were found guilty of first-degree murder. I did my best to defend my client, but that does not mean I disagreed with the verdict.

* * * * * * * *

I was retained to defend a more sympathetic client, although he was charged with a very serious crime, kidnapping for ransom. Four assailants entered the home of a local drug dealer who lived with his two sisters in Moreno Valley, California. The assailants, wearing ski masks, burglarized the residence, bound and blindfolded the sisters and moved them to the assailants' van. Messages were sent from the assailants to the sisters' family demanding ransom for their release. The money was to be dropped in a public park. The police were contacted and an investigation begun. Plainclothes officers entered the park in advance of the money drop. The neighboring streets were all monitored. The ransom money was retrieved by the assailants who were arrested on the spot. The SWAT team encircled and swooped down on a van parked on a neighboring street. The driver of the van was wearing a ski mask. Under his seat, a gun was found. He had jewelry in his pocket from the burglary of the victims' home. In the back of the van there were two women bound and blindfolded. The driver's name was Vincent Reyes. He was my client. He had never been in trouble before.

Vincent was 22 years old, a descendant of Central American Mayan Indians. He and his mother shared the same Native American facial features, particularly in their brown almond-shaped eyes, flat nose and high cheekbones. Mother's sweet face highlighted the tenderness underlying Vincent's rougher edges. The punishment for kidnapping for ransom is life without the possibility of parole. His mother was overwhelmed with fear, as her son was facing the most serious of charges. She hired me to help. With these facts, how could any lawyer help? Three defendants were charged with the crimes, all to be tried together. By the time the trial started, the defendants had been in custody two years. Pretrial motions and attorney unavailability caused the delays. The case was assigned to Judge Monica Lovell. I made sure my client's mother sat in the first row of the spectators' gallery for the entire trial, directly behind my client. Her proximity and kind, gentle features accentuated Vincent's mildness, in sharp contrast to the violent nature of the kidnapping. I also felt Mom's concern for her son would be evident to the jury. Sharing the same dignified features, mother and son faced the jury together.

The DA, Ted Sarkisian, a friend since my early DA years, presented his case. Because the DA had alleged the crime was committed in the furtherance of gang activity, he was able to present evidence of Vincent's "gang-related history." While Vincent had no prior convictions, he did have a nickname, "Maestro." The DA called a detective from the police gang unit to the stand. He told the jury that many gang members have gang names and that my client's moniker was Maestro. I asked if he was aware that my client was called Maestro because he was known as the "Mayan Maestro of Break Dance." The detective shook his head and smirked. Vincent would spend the rest of his life in prison and all this detective could do was smile smugly. Was it funny sending people to prison for the rest of their lives?

At the end of the DA's case, the judge asked if I had any witnesses. "I call the defendant, Vincent Reyes, to the witness stand." Vincent walked to the stand, took the oath and sat down. I asked, "Mr. Reyes, why do they call you Maestro?" He responded bashfully, "Because I am the Maestro of Break Dance." I asked, "Can you prove you are the Maestro of Break Dance?" "Sure," he replied. "Your honor, with the Court's permission, I request to have Mr. Reyes exit the witness stand and demonstrate to the jury why his moniker is Maestro." Of course, the DA objected. Prosecutors often object to any effort to humanize a defendant. Judge Lovell overruled, saying, "You raised the issue of the gang nickname. The defense can rebut it."

Vincent stepped down from the witness stand and started break dancing for the entire courtroom. He dropped to the floor, twisting his hips and legs to the right, then left. He swung his legs in a circle while balancing on his hands. He spun briefly on his head. He was embarrassed, but good. The jury laughed.

After the dance, Vincent retook the witness stand. He told the following story. He was in a public parking lot with friends. They were high. He had a boom box playing dance music, while he showed off his moves. A well-known gang leader drove up in a van and motioned for Vincent to come over. "I'll pay you to watch my van for a while," he said. Vincent agreed, mostly because he was afraid to say no. The gang leader told Vincent where they should meet and Vincent began walking to the location. Vincent showed the jury his steps drawn on a diagram of the route he had taken to meet the van. When he arrived at the location, Vincent stepped into the driver's side of the van and sat down. The gang leader gave him a handful of jewelry, which he accepted as payment, putting it into his pocket. After he entered the van, he saw the bound and blindfolded girls in the back. He panicked. If he left, the gang leader would kill him. If he stayed, he would be implicated as an accomplice to some heinous crime. He was young, intoxicated and simply did not know what to do. He noticed that on the passenger seat next to him somebody had left a ski mask. He compounded his mistakes and put it on, thinking at least nobody would know who he was. Within seconds, the SWAT team stormed the van and arrested him. By the time he finished testifying, the jury looked sympathetic. They had taken a liking to him because of the break dancing and his embarrassment at the silliness of his performance in such a public and serious situation.

Since kidnapping requires asportation (movement), I argued that Vincent could not be guilty of kidnapping because he did not transport the victims. I told the jury that Vincent made a serious error of judgment, but could not withdraw from the situation once the initial error was made. He did the best he could, given these horrible circumstances. If anything, I argued, Vincent was guilty of false imprisonment, but not kidnapping. I told them, if they felt it was important to convict him, it should be for false imprisonment only. The jury did not know that if convicted of this charge, Vincent had already served the maximum time. The jury acquitted on kidnapping and found him guilty of the lesser crime of false imprisonment. After two years in jail, arm in arm with his mother, Vincent walked out of the courtroom.

* * * * * * * *

In the mid-1990s, Riverside County, east of Los Angeles, was growing at a rate of thirty-two percent per year. The crime rate had skyrocketed and Riverside had outgrown its justice system. The courthouse was bursting at the seams. There was a great need for police officers, judges, probation officers, prosecutors and defense attorneys. I opened a third office in Riverside and started taking cases. I would often travel from my Los Angeles Arco Towers office, to my Alhambra office and then to Riverside.

I became friends with one of the Riverside judges, a proficient criminal calendar judge. She was cited for a traffic violation in Glendale and asked me to handle the matter. She offered to pay me, but knew I wouldn't take her money. I went to Glendale Court, pleaded not guilty and set a trial date. There are not many defenses for most traffic violations, so I try to pick a date when the traffic officer is more likely not to appear, such as a day immediately before or after a holiday. Twenty percent of the time the officer does not show up for one reason or another. In this case, the officer did not appear. Since most courts give attorneys priority, the commissioner called my case first. The commissioner remarked that since the officer was not present, the case would have to be continued. I told the belligerent commissioner that I was ready for trial and did not agree to a continuance. He said I had to agree since the officer was not in court. I said we had the right to a speedy trial under the law and I wanted to start immediately. The commissioner retorted he was sorry, but we could not have a trial this day and he would continue it. We went on in this vein for ten minutes, as my frustration and anger grew. Finally he said, "Case dismissed." The commissioner had no idea that my client was a Superior Court Judge in Riverside County. When I told the judge her case was dismissed, she said, "How did you do it?" I looked at her mysteriously, "You don't want to know." When my wife, Jia-Ning, and I had our first child, the judge sent baby clothes.

In Riverside, I was appointed to represent Wilhelm Montoya, a long-time criminal. Montoya had been in and out of prison much of his adult life. He was accused of killing a government informant. Montoya had a good friend, a woman charged with running a meth lab. The woman was part of a local group of friends, all with extensive criminal records, who injected methamphetamine. A government informant was set to testify against this woman at her upcoming trial. Witnesses later testified they overheard conversations in which the woman complained to Montoya about the informant and his impending testimony. One night the informant was shot to death as he lay asleep in his car. A witness heard four gunshots. The victim was discovered by his mother in the driver's seat of his vehicle parked in a dirt turnout across the street from her house. The day after the murder, Montoya was overheard telling his friend that he had taken care of her problem, "You don't have nothin' to worry about no more."

We went to trial. The witnesses for the DA testified against Montoya and spoke about his connection to the informant and Montoya's relationship with the woman running the meth lab. Witnesses said that Montoya would watch the informant with binoculars from his home. Montoya was charged with two special circumstances: lying in wait and killing a witness to a crime. Montoya, a short, portly, balding man, had tattoos of SS seared over portions of his body. SS referred to the villainous German paramilitary which carried out the Holocaust. While half Latino, his fair complexion resembled that of his German mother's. After proving to gang leaders his hatred of his Guatemalan father, and all Latinos for that matter, he was allegedly accepted into the Aryan Brotherhood. Montoya was reputed to have an SS tattoo for each person he had murdered. Despite the awful facts of the alleged murder and my disdain for Montoya's repulsive affiliation with a neo-Nazi clan, I did my best to help him. However, an unsympathetic judge, a conservative jury and the weight of the evidence contributed to a conviction of first-degree murder, with the special circumstance of "lying in wait." The court sentenced Montoya to life in prison without the possibility of parole.

* * * * * * * *

Montoya's SS tattoos were reminiscent of history's infamous German mass murderers. My very next trial, in contrast, involved an innocent, loving German wife and mother, killed in Southern California. I was ordered to begin trial on this high profile, special circumstance murder, labeled by the media as the "German Tourist Slaying Case." In an earlier German tourist case, September 1993, Mr. Hermann Swalbenberg, a 33-year-old mechanical engineer from a small town outside Hamburg, looked forward to touring Miami with his pregnant wife. Minutes after landing, his rental car was rammed by two men in a van. As Swalbenberg continued driving, the van pulled alongside and he was shot to death, the fourth German killed that year in Florida during an attempted robbery. Berlin's newspaper, *Tagesspiel*, headlined, "Another German Killed in Miami."

In May, 1994, a German tourist was murdered in Idyllic Trails, California. Idyllic Trails is a mountain paradise, drawing tourists from all over the world. Gertrude Strauss, 64, and her husband Hans were vacationing in Southern California, visiting their daughter. During their stay, They drove to Idyllic Trails to enjoy hiking the pristine pathways,

While at Idyllic Trails, two assailants approached them. One stole Mrs. Strauss's purse. When she fought back, she was shot in the head with a .380 caliber semi-automatic handgun. When her husband came to her aid, he was shot in the face and wounded. He would live, but would never be the same. In addition to losing his wife, his speech was permanently impaired. Three men were involved. My client was not accused of being the actual shooter, but instead, helping plan and carry out the robberies.

The trial began. During *voir dire*, the questioning of the jury, the DA told a story about his three daughters. The three of them conspired to steal cookies from the cookie jar. The two youngest girls pushed the kitchen chair to the countertop. The oldest girl stood on the chair, reached into the cookie jar and removed a cookie for each. All three, he said, were guilty of stealing the cookies and they each had to be punished equally, even though the two youngest girls only pushed the chair to the counter. Then he asked the jurors if any of them disagreed with the law on aiding and abetting. In my *voir dire*, I told the jury I was new to Riverside and did not know many people in the area. But I did make some friends, one of whom was a DA who invited me to his house for supper. I went to his home and witnessed a curious event. When he and his wife stepped out of the room, I watched his three daughters raid the cookie jar. When the two younger girls pushed the chair, I noticed the youngest, the cutest of all, say, "I don't think we should be doing this. Daddy will be mad." She stopped. When Dad found out about the cookies, even though the little one had withdrawn from the cookie theft, he punished all three girls. Then I asked if the jury could follow the Court's instructions relating to the laws regarding intent and withdrawal from criminal activity. Using the same story, both lawyers were guilty of arguing their respective positions during jury selection, a process where argument is not permitted.

When arrested, the police told my client they already knew about his involvement in the crime. Because of recurrent forest fires, cameras had been installed in the trees. The murder was caught on videotape. My naive client believed it and confessed. Of course, no such cameras existed. My client's confession included a self-serving statement that he tried to withdraw from the criminal activity before the shooting, although he was not able to prevent the crime. Having no other defense, I would use this to argue he lacked the requisite intent to commit the crime.

The husband flew in from Germany and testified how he lost his wife in the blink of an eye. On the witness stand, when asked if he could identify the assailants, he pointed at my client and shouted, *"Swinehund!"* I resisted the urge to hide under counsel table. The officer testified next, detailing my client's confession. My client was convicted. At sentencing, I presented over twenty family members and friends to testify regarding his laudable character and responsible behavior at home. The judge concluded, "The evil you did on this one occasion outweighs by mountains, all the good you've done in your life put together."

* * * * * * * *

Criminal defense lawyers measure success differently than most people. For example, when a defendant is facing three consecutive life terms and the attorney reaches a twenty-year plea deal, the attorney has achieved a good disposition. While it looks dire for the client who will spend his next twenty years in prison, at least he will eventually be released. Sometimes the evidence against a defendant is so overwhelming, there is simply no way out. By keeping a client from life in prison, a criminal defense attorney would consider such disposition a success, even though an ordinary person might call it a failure.

At any given time, I had over twenty life-in-prison cases pending while maintaining an office in Riverside. In a retrial of a murder case, Gordon Smiggly had previously been convicted of first-degree murder and was sentenced to twenty-five years to life in prison. The appellate court reversed the conviction, citing prosecutorial misconduct, due to the DA's overzealous and misleading closing argument. In an effort to show how "magnanimous" he was, the prosecutor punished

Mr. Smiggly by adding special circumstance murder charges, meaning Smiggly was now facing life without the possibility of parole, listing as the special circumstance that the murder was committed in the course of a robbery.

I filed a motion to dismiss the special circumstance, based on a theory of vindictive prosecution. There had been no changes in any of the evidence. The circumstances and evidence were exactly the same since the original filing of the case. No new witnesses came forward. It appeared the only reason the charges were increased was to punish Smiggly for appealing. I called the Deputy DA handling the case to the witness stand and questioned him about the decision to file the more serious allegation. He testified that the special circumstance should have been filed previously and was only left out in error. The judge agreed and allowed the special circumstance to stand.

The judge later told me the trial was a "slugfest." Attacking and weaving like prizefighters, the DA and I punched and counterpunched with our examinations. My client had gone to the crime scene with the shooter, who was convicted of this murder several years earlier. The DA called the shooter to the witness stand. His testimony was all over the place, initially refusing to admit any wrongdoing, protecting himself. Later he tried to defend Smiggly. This muddled the already messy trial. Smiggly's defense was that, while he did go to the crime scene, he did not know about the gun and the shooter's plan to kill the woman. He had no intent to participate in a robbery or murder and was not present in the room when the woman was shot. Later, after the woman was killed, Smiggly did participate in a burglary of the house. Further, he did nothing to help the woman after she had been shot. This was a tricky defense, because it showed that Smiggly had no empathy for the victim.

I argued to the jury that the DA had not proven Smiggly was part of the murder and was not present, having gone to the bathroom when the shooter actually killed the woman. Deadlocked, the jury could not reach a verdict. Smiggly had previously been convicted of first-degree murder with a sentence of twenty-five years to life. Because the jury hung, the judge declared a mistrial. Before a retrial began, the DA offered to resolve the case as a second degree murder, reducing Smiggly's exposure from life without the possibility of parole on the special circumstance, or twenty-five to life on a straight first degree murder, to fifteen to life for second degree murder. My client jumped at the deal. He will be eligible for parole ten years earlier due to this disposition.

* * * * * * * *

Like the critic who accused me of being immoral because I am a criminal defense lawyer, Professor Adil Randeep never imagined he would need one. A Ph.D. in Electrical Engineering from Mumbai, India, Dr. Randeep lived in an upscale neighborhood in Long Beach. Very late one night, he was awakened by a loud noise. Thinking someone had broken into his home, he grabbed a gun he kept for protection. He sprang out of bed and started searching the house. Some years earlier a man had attempted to break through his four-year-old daughter's bedroom window with a hammer. The police came that time but the burglar had run away.

On this night, a drunk driver swerved into his front yard and crashed into his home. After Dr. Randeep realized the sound came from outside, half naked, he went to his front porch and observed a car smashed into his house. He yelled to his wife, "Call 911." Someone was sitting in the car furtively moving about, acting strangely. Dr. Randeep aimed the gun at the man and said, "Get out of the car so I can see your hands." Dr. Randeep was worried the man had a weapon. The driver of the car was told to kneel on the ground with his arms behind his back and wait for the police to arrive. But the man would not follow orders. Flailing his arms, he kept running around the car. To prove the gun was loaded, Dr. Randeep first fired into the ground. Then to show the bullets were real and not blanks, he fired into the car's headlight. The driver eventually knelt down and put his hands behind his back to wait for the police.

Officers came and arrested Dr. Randeep for shooting into the vehicle and brandishing a firearm. Dr. Randeep, an upstanding member of the community and prominent university professor, never had any negative contacts with law enforcement. After he was arrested, he hired me and I fought the case through jury trial. The prosecutor was insistent on Dr. Randeep going to jail for six months. At trial, the victim testified he drank only a little alcohol, lost control of his vehicle and crashed into the house. He testified Dr. Randeep threatened him with the gun and shot into his car. While the victim was testifying, I noticed his gang-styled baggy pants. I asked him about the chain hanging out of his back pocket, and he said, "It holds my wallet." Pulling out the wallet, he displayed a long, thick, intimidating metal chain. Watching the jury carefully, I said, "It looks like you're carrying a weapon." He responded, "I guess it could be." He had a wise guy attitude.

I obtained a copy of the victim's police report. He had been arrested at the scene for drunk driving, for which he later pleaded guilty. When he testified that he was not intoxicated, I impeached him with the police report and the fact that he pleaded guilty to drunk driving. He appeared to be lying about not being intoxicated.

Dr. Randeep nervously testified from the witness stand. He continuously reminded the jury that he was scared that night, because in the past someone had broken into his daughter's room. "After hearing the crash, the first thing I told my wife was to call 911. I kept thinking of the prior incident and how I feared somebody was trying to kidnap my daughter. All I wanted to do was to keep the assailant there until the police came."

There is a presumption under California law that a person acts in self-defense when an intruder appears in his or her home. I had asked for a jury instruction on this presumption, but the judge refused, saying that in this case, the intruder had never actually entered the house. I did some research, filed a brief and changed the judge's mind. In closing argument, I told the jury that protecting one's home is natural. A wild animal threatened in the jungle will run away. Confronted near its home, it will fight to the death. The jury found the professor not guilty.

* * * * * * * *

Proposition 115, the Crime Victim's Justice Reform Act, became law in 1990, allowing police officers to testify to hearsay evidence under certain circumstances at preliminary hearings. It relieved victims and witnesses of appearing in court after giving statements to a Proposition 115 certified police officer. Hearsay is any statement made out of court to prove the truth of what has been stated. After Proposition 115, officers could testify for witnesses not present in court. The judge was required to hear the testimony, despite a hearsay objection.

My former colleague from the DA's office in West Covina, Andrew Garvin, was now a member of the District Attorney's

Hardcore Gang Unit. Prior to the passage of Proposition 115, Andrew prosecuted a gang murder case. At the preliminary hearing, Garvin called witnesses whose testimony was so obviously incredible and unreliable, the court refused to hold the defendant to answer to the charge.

After having the case dismissed at an earlier preliminary hearing, and knowing that Proposition 115 had since become law, Garvin re-filed the charges and a new preliminary hearing was set in front of a different judicial officer, Judge Marilyn Stanislaus. In the new preliminary hearing, Garvin called his investigating detective to the stand. He had the detective testify under Proposition 115 to the hearsay statements of the same witnesses who had testified at the original preliminary hearing. Garvin did not call any of these witnesses to testify at this proceeding. I inquired of the detective on cross-examination if he was present at the first preliminary hearing. He responded he was. I asked if he heard the witnesses testify on direct and cross-examination and he said he had. I questioned if he discovered any new evidence since that time and he said he had not. I asked the witness if he was present when the judge ruled there was not sufficient evidence to hold the defendant to answer. He said yes. I stopped. I looked at Judge Stanislaus who was staring incredulously at Garvin. She asked him if he was serious about presenting this case, which had no new evidence and was previously dismissed, based on a finding of witness non-credibility. Garvin insisted he had the right under Proposition 115 to do so. Judge Stanislaus disagreed and summarily dismissed the case.

* * * * * * * *

In another preliminary hearing, I represented Arturo Marinero, a member of a Latino gang. In a South Los Angeles street battle, a rival gang member aimed a shotgun point-blank at Arturo and pulled the trigger. The gun jammed and Arturo wrestled the firearm away, knocking the rival down with the butt of the shotgun. A female witness observed the incident and watched Arturo discard the gun before the two gang members fled in opposite directions. The woman soon heard gunshots. The man Arturo knocked down had been shot and killed. The woman identified Arturo as the one who took the shotgun away from the man. Arturo was arrested.

I appeared at the arraignment, pleaded not guilty and set the matter for a preliminary hearing within the statutory time. Since Arturo was in custody, the statutory time in which he had the right to a preliminary hearing was ten court days. At the preliminary hearing, the female witness testified about the fight and how Arturo took the gun from the rival. On cross-examination, she admitted that while Arturo had full control of the gun he had wrestled away, Arturo never aimed it at the victim. She also indicated that after Arturo ran away, the victim stood and ran in the opposite direction. Just seconds later, she heard the shots that killed the victim. It was clear from her testimony that of all the gang members present, Arturo was the only one who could not have been the murderer. He had just run full speed in the opposite direction from where the victim was killed. However, the preliminary hearing judge decided there was enough evidence for probable cause and held Arturo to answer to the charges. It did not matter. The DA now understood the serious weaknesses in his case.

In the days that followed, I had discussions with the DA. I reiterated that the preliminary hearing testimony proved Arturo was the only person at the scene we could say with complete certainty did not commit the murder. The more I argued, the more he agreed. Arturo stayed in custody while the DA thought about the situation. I filed a motion to dismiss the case in a higher court, and a hearing on that motion occurred thirty days later. The DA, too uncomfortable to proceed but not willing to dismiss the case, did not oppose the judge's tentative grant of my motion. The judge dismissed the case.

* * * * * * * *

I resolved yet another murder case in a dismissal without the need for trial. Mr. Fred Lott suffered extreme back pain. He had multiple surgeries to correct the problem, but none succeeded. His only relief was medication, and given the duration of his pain, his tolerance for medication grew, resulting in the need for more and more potent drugs. His doctor wanted to wean him off the drugs, but Lott insisted he needed them. Eventually, his doctor refused further prescriptions. Lott, still in terrible pain, turned to self-medicating by purchasing street drugs such as heroin. This went on far too long, and wanting to end his addiction to pain medication, Lott began a program of treatment at a local methadone clinic. Many of the participants in the program were ordered there by the Court or Probation Department. Lott was there of his own free will. One of the patients at the clinic sold heroin and other drugs in the parking lot. Where better to market such products? When Lott learned of this, he told the clinic's administrators who contacted the police and had the man arrested.

The drug dealer was gone for a while, presumably in jail, and returned to his sales job some months later in the same parking lot. Leaving from the clinic on a warm July day, Lott heard someone yell, "There's the guy who turned you in." As Lott entered his car, four assailants surrounded the vehicle: the drug dealer in front, one in back and one on either side. The drug dealer held a container of liquid in his hands and poured it on the windshield. Lott had spent many years teaching safe driving as a certified traffic school instructor and would not move the car without clearing the windshield, which was now covered in an opaque liquid.

Approximately ten years earlier, Lott had been the victim of a home invasion robbery. He had been beaten, hog-tied, blindfolded, rolled up in a rug and left for dead, resulting in permanent damage to his back. Since that time, he carried a knife in his car. Lott tried using the windshield wipers, but they only smeared the substance making visibility worse. Knife in hand, Lott exited his car to wipe the windshield with a rag so he could drive away. The drug dealer attacked. Then the others joined in, pummeling him. Thrusting the knife toward the drug dealer in an effort to push him back, Lott stabbed the man directly through the heart. Mortally wounded, he collapsed, blood pouring from his chest. The three other assailants fled. There were many witnesses yelling at Lott to run away before the police came. He would not. Instead, Lott cried out, "Call 911, call the paramedics." While paramedics were en route, Lott took off his jacket and put it on top of the dying man, hoping to avoid his going into shock. Paramedics arrived and administered first aid, to no avail. The police appeared and arrested Lott for murder. Held in jail, his bail was set at a million dollars, the customary bail for murder. His family retained me.

I contacted the DA handling the case and spoke with him about the facts. He agreed this was an unusual case and that, while it might not have risen to the level of murder, he believed he could prove manslaughter. Sometimes the DA files murder charges even when it is obviously manslaughter and lets the jury sort it out. I argued that no crime was committed and that a case for self-defense had never been clearer. Ever since Lott was left for dead rolled up in a rug, he has been claustrophobic. Being in jail was torture to him. I reasoned with the DA, that if he really believed this to be a case of manslaughter, then at least agree that bail be set at the schedule for manslaughter, at the time $80,000. He agreed, bail was set, a bond was posted and Lott was freed pending the outcome of the proceedings.

Lott was haunted by the prospect of returning to jail. I felt he would likely kill himself if incarcerated again. He pressured me to defend him in such a way that he would never have to return to custody. He asked me to take no risks. The immediate problem was solved. He was out of jail and I set my sights on defending him. I sent an investigator to take statements from the witnesses. Initially, we obtained a half dozen statements of eyewitnesses who confirmed Lott was being pounded by the four assailants at the time of the stabbing. I also had toxicology reports from the decedent's autopsy showing he was under the influence of cocaine at the time. In order to explain why Lott had a knife, I obtained a copy of the ten-year-old police report of the home-invasion robbery where Lott was left for dead. I gathered letters verifying Lott's good character and his traffic school teaching certificates. I put all this information in a report and gave it to the DA in an effort to get the case dismissed.

The DA was sympathetic to some extent, but held his position that manslaughter had occurred. I believed the case was completely defensible. But to prove self-defense, we would have to go to trial, which always entails risk. Lott was adamant about not jeopardizing his freedom. I felt my hands were tied and that I had to negotiate a settlement that avoided any further incarceration. The DA was willing to leave the sentencing entirely up to the judge, but wanted Lott to plead guilty to manslaughter. I hated the prospect of pleading guilty on these facts, but Lott was the client, and after all, it was his life.

The DA agreed that if we were to plead guilty, I could choose the judge. I had Judge Jack Leira in mind, a former police lieutenant and one of the most decent, honest and fair judges on the bench. Before we entered this plea agreement, I insisted on talking to the judge to see if he would be amenable to sentencing Lott to straight probation on a manslaughter charge. This would be a very rare disposition, since there was a dead body and a guilty plea to manslaughter. It would take tremendous courage for a judge to give straight probation. Ordinarily, felony manslaughter results in a prison commitment of many years. But this was truly an odd situation.

The DA and I visited the judge in chambers. Judge Leira understood both our positions. He intimated that based on our representations, he would be open to resolving the case in such a way that would result in no further incarceration, so long as the defendant satisfactorily complied with probation, which I knew would not be a problem. The judge said he would need a compelling pre-sentencing report. He wanted solid evidence upon which to base his decision. He gave me three weeks to prepare the report and we set a date for a change of plea. I had earlier given a report to the DA's office, but now I acquired additional evidence. I obtained further toxicology and psychiatric reports of the aggressive effects of the drugs in the decedent's body. I obtained the decedent's arrest record, filled with drug arrests and crimes of violence. I added more character and eyewitness letters. I put together a comprehensive pre-sentencing report so the judge had plenty to rely on in sentencing the client to straight probation with no additional incarceration.

I submitted my pre-sentencing report a week before we were set to enter the new plea. At this point, my goal was to ensure Lott did not return to custody. I believed the pre-sentencing report would do just that. On the day before we were due to plead, I received a call from the second-in-command of the DA's office in the branch where the case was pending. I had known this high-ranking DA since even before I was a Deputy District Attorney. He told me he read the pre-sentencing report and that his office was no longer comfortable accepting a plea of guilty to manslaughter from Lott. The following day the DA's office dismissed the case.

* * * * * * * *

Criminal defense lawyers are trained to carefully examine the facts and details of the incident leading to the client's arrest. The specifics of the crime are usually described in crime reports prepared by police officers. The descriptions in these reports often lack sufficient detail to capture the totality of the evidence. Defense attorneys do not merely rely on these crime reports when devising the defense strategy, but often participate in a thorough independent investigation. Nothing replaces the hands-on knowledge one gains from personally talking to a witness, viewing the crime scene and noticing firsthand the lighting, distances and witnesses' demeanors. Criminal lawyers hire defense investigators to assist in trial preparation. Most investigators are former sheriff deputies or police officers who have retired and work part-time.

On a fraud case in 2006, I hired a Spanish-speaking investigator to assist me in a Latino part of town, where we needed to photograph certain houses. This investigator and I drove to South Central Los Angeles and began photographing houses and talking with some of the residents. As we stood in the street, a shirtless, muscular Latino man in his early 30s approached us, his powerful upper body covered with tattoos. He told us we were on his street and that we had not asked his permission to be there and take photographs. The investigator and I were both wearing suits and ties. Usually a well-dressed stranger appearing in this neighborhood is a police detective or works for the government. The street thugs will ordinarily stay away from such professionals. This hoodlum decided to target us for extortion. He said we needed his okay to take photographs on his territory. I responded that I represented one of his homeboys who would be happy we were there taking care of his case. I said we were finishing up and would be leaving. At that point, my investigator, a former police officer, walked up to the man, jutting his chin into the thug's face and barked, "Get the fuck out of our way; we don't need your fucking permission to be on a city street." This was unnecessarily confrontational. We did not know if this gangster had reinforcements nearby. I put my hand on the investigator's shoulder and said, "We're done." Pushing him back to the car, I told him we were leaving. Once inside, he reached into his glove compartment and took out a semi-automatic handgun, pulling back the slide. I immediately yelled at him to put the gun away. Seeing the stone look on my face, he complied. He put the car into reverse and drove backward a city block to avoid the gang member. When we arrived at my office, I thanked the investigator and advised him I would no longer need his services.

My next murder case was dismissed pretrial after a thorough defense investigation proved my client innocent. Peter Czerny worked in Beverly Hills selling maps to stars' homes. He was a twenty-year-old immigrant from Turkey, likeable but a little goofy. He had never been arrested before. He was on his way to work one day when he stopped for a soda at a 7-Eleven. He met and chatted with a charismatic young man called Markos, who asked Peter for a ride. Markos suggested Peter take the day off and hang out with Markos and his friends.

Markos took Peter to a run-down hotel where his friends stayed. He led Peter to a fifth floor room where other residents of the hotel were partying, smoking marijuana and drinking. Peter partied the rest of the night while Markos "borrowed his car." Peter was a sociable kid and the hotel guests welcomed him. One of the partiers was nicknamed *Hombre Colombiano*. Peter smoked and drank all night, falling asleep on a stack of clothes in a closet. When he awoke the next morning, Markos and Peter's car were gone. Peter left and walked around the neighborhood. Several hours later, he found his unlocked car parallel parked on the street. Without keys, he sat in the driver's seat trying to figure out what to do. A man in a wheelchair rode up and asked Peter if he could lie in the backseat and rest. Peter helped him in. The man told of witnessing a murder the previous night. Twenty feet from the parked car, an assailant had stabbed a man to death.

Across the street two brothers, ages thirteen and fourteen, looked out their third floor apartment window and saw the "murderer" return to his car. They called the police who arrested Peter for murder. The man in the wheelchair told the police they were apprehending the wrong person. They disregarded his comments, thinking he was deliberately trying to protect his friend.

Peter spent eight months in county jail before I was appointed to take over his case. The DA was Kelvin Burnside. "You know, Sandy," he said, "I've been watching this kid come to court for months now and he does not appear violent." Despite his observations, Kelvin said the arrest reports looked bad. These reports included Peter's statement that he had met Markos and partied at the hotel, that Markos had borrowed his car, that he found the car and met the man in the wheelchair who had witnessed the murder.

Knowing his gang name was Markos made it easy to find an old booking photo. In reviewing the police reports, I was surprised there was no identification or statement from the man in the wheelchair. I made an informal discovery request seeking the Field Identification (FI) cards. Any time there is a crime, the police will ask everyone in the vicinity for basic contact information, which is recorded on an index card. The prosecution turned over about twenty-five of these FI cards from the original investigation. I started calling the phone numbers. The tenth call was a hit. I told the man on the other line that I was a lawyer investigating a murder and I was looking for a wheelchair-bound witness with whom I needed to speak. The man said, "You are looking for my son, Jordan." I scheduled a time to meet. The next day, at King's Donuts on Virgil Street and Beverly Boulevard, Jordan told me the whole story, emphatically declaring that he had been telling the detectives for eight months they had the wrong guy.

I visited the shabby hotel where Peter and Markos had partied. I spoke with the manager and asked for the names of the residents who were staying on the fifth floor the date of the murder. I wanted to find *Hombre Colombiano*. The manager gave me a list of five names. He said he heard some of them were in jail. I took the names to the county jail where the sheriffs kept a thick book listing inmates' booking numbers and locations. This was before the county had an online system. One of the names matched. I took a court-certified Spanish interpreter and went to see the inmate. He was an older man. I related the story and showed him Peter's photograph. I told him I was looking for *Hombre Colombiano*. With a wide grin, he said, "That's me." He looked at the picture of Peter and conveyed much of the same information as Peter did. I showed him the picture of Markos. "Do you know this man?" He studied me carefully, and then looked away. It was obvious he knew the truth. "Hombre, if you don't tell the truth, Peter's going to spend the rest of his life in prison." He nodded at Peter's photograph, and then put his hand on his heart. He pointed to Markos's picture and gestured, suggesting not to ask, as he would be afraid to say.

I gave a copy of the witness statements to Kelvin. He assigned one of his trial deputies to review the matter. She and her investigator accompanied me for a second meeting with *Hombre Colombiano* who confirmed what he had told me. They met with Jordan, who advised them he had been telling the detectives for eight months they had arrested the wrong man. The detectives never made a report of Jordan's statement. Unknown to me, the DA investigator displayed two "six packs" to the eyewitnesses, the two boys who called the police, because the "murderer" had returned to his car. "Six packs" are folders holding six photographs of similar looking men. One six pack contained Peter's photo, one Markos's. Having watched Peter in the car, the younger boy remembered Peter. The older brother confidently picked out Markos as the murderer. It was enough. Kelvin dismissed the case.

* * * * * * * *

Mel Goldfarb referred me a kidnapping case in Northern California. The victim, a Cambodian immigrant with criminal ties, accused my client of appearing at his home to demand payment of money owed. According to the victim, the situation escalated when my client denied he owed the money. My client allegedly broke the man's shoulder after violently throwing him to the ground. The victim alleged that my unarmed client kidnapped and forced him into his own car, drove him to a crowded restaurant, where they drank tea and ate dim sum. When filing the kidnapping charge, one wonders what was in the mind of the supervising Deputy DA. Imagine a forcible, violent kidnapping of an adult where the hiding place is a crowded public restaurant. Why didn't the filing DA ask the obvious questions, "How could this broken-shouldered victim be kidnapped and taken to such a public place? Wouldn't it be easy to tell a waiter, a fellow customer, a busboy, to call the police?" Instead, he spent an hour with the suspect and then left on his own. I never heard of a kidnapping with such ridiculous facts. This didn't stop the DA from filing the charges. Kidnapping, under California Penal Code Section 207, is punishable by a maximum of eight years in state prison.

I fought the case and vigorously cross-examined the victim at the preliminary hearing. I asked all those questions the filing DA did not. My inquiry was designed to illustrate the absurdity of the charges. "How crowded was the restaurant? Were you able to communicate with the waiter or the other patrons? You did not ask the waiter to call the police? You did not ask other patrons to call the police? You did not stand up and announce you were being kidnapped?" At the end of the preliminary hearing, the DA argued that, despite the weird circumstances, the victim testified to the elements of the crime and that for preliminary hearing purposes, there was sufficient evidence. The judge agreed. The case lingered for a year. Thereafter, no DA wanted to try this case. They just kept postponing it. I had many conversations with the filing DA and finally on the eve of trial, they dismissed the case. My client, thoroughly exhausted from the process, was grateful.

* * * * * * * *

Sometimes serious crimes are committed due to mental illness, and not from evil intent. I received a call from a woman in Chicago that her son, Tyler Washington, was in custody. She detailed his repeated and frightening episodes of schizophrenia. Accused of brandishing a hammer in a rude and threatening manner, Tyler sat on a concrete bench inside the holding tank next to Department 30 in the Criminal Courts Building. His eyes darted wildly as he told me the CIA was secretly videotaping him, broadcasting his every move to a European audience. He pointed to his back molars where the "CIA had inserted listening devices." Tyler was completely irrational and difficult to deal with. I needed to involve a psychiatrist, so I postponed the case until I could get him examined. He stayed in custody pending the next court date. In the meantime, I spoke to medical personnel at the jail about getting him medication that could help his mental condition. After calls from the defense psychiatrist, Tyler was given the appropriate medications. When he was lucid, I talked him into pleading no contest to a misdemeanor charge with a sentence of probation requiring continued psychiatric treatment and no additional jail time.

Most criminal defense lawyers see such cases throughout their careers. Clients say the government is monitoring them, secretly implanting listening devices on them, in the mouth, feet, back, arms or shoulders. They will insist they can hear the government whispering to them.

In contrast to Tyler's lifetime struggle with mental illness, Jerry Flood was on top of the world. He had recently worked as a play-by-play sportscaster for a major league soccer team. Earlier in his career, he was a well-known sports reporter with his own evening show. In addition, he had written award-winning sports programs. He knew and had interviewed many of the world's most famous athletes. When I met him, he was in jail, arrested for kidnapping and assaulting a young boy.

Several days earlier, he was in a large department store, grabbed a young boy, wrestled with the boy's mother and attempted to drag the boy away. While wrestling over the boy, Jerry was screaming wildly, incoherently. I was hired after his arrest.

I visited Jerry at the hospital ward of the jail. This was the first time in his life he had experienced such bizarre and delusional symptoms. Because of the charges and the abnormally inappropriate behavior, Jerry's bail was set at $250,000, well beyond his means. After visiting him at the jail, I immediately hired a psychiatrist. I appeared in court with Jerry, pleaded not guilty and asked for a bail hearing as soon as possible, which the judge calendared five days later. I prepared a bail motion and detailed Jerry's long and eventful career. In addition, I presented a psychiatric report explaining the exact illness, his prognosis and the recommendation of a special clinic, which would treat him back to health. Clean, safe and comfortable, the clinic was supervised twenty-four hours a day. I submitted with my motion a videotape of Jerry's famous interviews which the judge watched. The psychiatrist assured the court that a recurrence of the erratic behavior would not happen if Jerry continued taking the appropriate medication. The judge agreed to release Jerry on the condition he reside at the treatment center.

Because of the delusional episode, Jerry was scared to death. He was horrified at what he was alleged to have done, but also worried since the DA wanted a five-year prison term. While the act in the department store was frightening, it was not the result of an evil state of mind. An insanity plea was out of the question since, if adjudged insane, Jerry could spend the rest of his life in a mental hospital. My goal was to resolve the case for a probationary sentence, one that allowed Jerry to stay in treatment, get healthy and rejoin society. This was difficult given the nature of the charges and the gratuitously harsh manner of the DA who would not consider anything I had to say. To him, I was just an immoral defense attorney. He was dealing with a man who committed a kidnapping, and kidnapping required state prison for as long as possible.

I attempted a variety of legal tactics to get the case dismissed. I tried over and over to talk to the DA. Nothing worked. The DA stubbornly demanded state prison, and the case proceeded toward trial. I had a sympathetic judge in this court, who understood the defendant's problems and prognosis, but even the judge was powerless to dismiss the case or even change the charges. That power relied solely with the District Attorney's Office. If we were to try the case, the matter would be transferred to a different court.

Keeping Jerry out of state prison was the primary objective. I decided I would buy as much time as possible. Each month, I sent the judge psychiatric reports detailing Jerry's progress. We watched him for eight months while his mental health improved. The DA was intransigent. The case was now old and the judge was pushing for a resolution. Avoiding trial was my goal as I feared losing and Jerry being sent to prison. At a pretrial hearing, I suggested an "open plea" to the court and asked how the judge would sentence him. "Pleading open" means admitting all the allegations in the charging document without an agreement from the prosecutor. Sometimes this is called "pleading to the sheet." The judge asked the DA for his comments, who responded by angrily insisting on state prison. The judge addressed us, "If he pleads open, I'll give him one year in the county jail, which can be served at the clinic where he is staying, including credit for the time he has already done and three years' probation." Jerry accepted this disposition.

I hope the DA never has a loved one in trouble facing such a callous prosecutor.

* * * * * * * *

Attorneys must have an intimate knowledge of the facts, as well as thoroughly understand the law as it applies to each unique set of circumstances. As new laws are passed and enforced, there is often little or no precedent to guide practitioners and judges. In its infancy, the California Three-Strikes Law was a perfect example.

In the early 90's, Perry Chappell participated in a bar room brawl. He was arrested and charged with assault with a deadly weapon and mayhem. He allegedly smashed a broken beer bottle into a victim, leaving a huge circular-shaped scar, hence the mayhem charge, willful mutilation of another's body. I worked out a unique deal to keep him out of state prison: formal felony probation with one year in county jail, served as work furlough. He had to plead guilty to both charges. The more serious mayhem charge could be dismissed at the expiration of his probation, pursuant to California Penal Code Section 1385, a dismissal for all purposes in the interest of justice. Usually a 1385 dismissal occurs at the time of a guilty plea. For example, when someone is charged with multiple counts, he pleads guilty to some of them. The others are dismissed 1385, in the interests of justice. In contrast, a defendant by a showing of good behavior may have his or her case dismissed pursuant to California Penal Code Section 1203.4, a rehabilitation statute. A 1385 dismissal is not the result of rehabilitation and does not require a purpose other than being in the interest of justice.

Both the assault with a deadly weapon and the mayhem counts against my client were serious felonies. At the time

Chappell pleaded guilty, California had no Three-Strikes Law. After California passed the Three-Strikes Law, his convictions seemingly gave him two strikes. With another felony conviction, he would be punished by twenty-five years to life in prison. Chappell was arrested for a new felony and charged with a third strike. I argued to the court that both priors were not valid strikes. The judge agreed to discharge the assault with a deadly weapon prior, but not the mayhem prior. As a second strike, Chappell was looking at two times the punishment on the new case, eighty percent of his sentence to be served in prison. My goal was to get the mayhem prior stricken. I was confident the 1385 mayhem dismissal could not be used as a strike. To date, there had been no appellate cases on point. The DA offered the low term of two years times two, due to the prior strike at eighty percent of time to be served. Ordinarily under California law, a plea of guilty results in the loss of one's appellate rights. In this case, I convinced the Court that, based on the absence of applicable appellate decisions, the judge should allow us to appeal the strike issue. He agreed and issued a Certificate of Probable Cause to appeal. Eleven months later, the appellate court ruled in our favor, and having served his time, Chappell was released from prison. This appellate opinion was the first of its kind in California relating to the Three-Strikes Law and Penal Code Section 1385 dismissals. I did not realize it at the time, but it had enormous consequences relative to deportation issues on my immigration cases.

Six months after I received notice of the successful appeal, I attended an immigration seminar, given by Franklin Russell, the leading expert on immigration consequences of criminal convictions. Several hundred lawyers attended the seminar. Russell spoke about a new California appellate case relating to California Penal Code Section 1385 dismissals of prior strikes and how such a disposition could now be used as a defense in removal proceedings. He was talking about my case. At the break, I approached Russell and told him I was the lawyer for the case he just cited. We talked about it for a while. The case is widely used today.

* * * * * * * *

California's strike law was also at issue in the Larry Adams case. His father explained the boy's mother had washed her hands of Larry because of his rebellious attitude and myriad legal scrapes. She would no longer help. Larry had been a troubled child, never finishing high school. His father too would wash his hands clean of the son, but the DA demanded Larry serve fifteen years in state prison and that "just wasn't fair." If Dad walked away now, he could not live with himself. He came to me, thinking I could make a difference. I spoke about the case with Dad who related his son was charged with multiple counts of robbery and burglary. As a juvenile, the son had a prior arson strike. I told the father I was reluctant to take the case because I was not sure I could help. The situation looked bleak, but Dad needed my help and paid the fee.

At the Public Defender's Office, I met with the attorney who had been representing the eighteen-year-old boy. I filed a "Substitution of Attorney" with the Court and gave a copy to the Public Defender who handed me the client's file. I reviewed the police reports, court records and the preliminary hearing transcripts on the current case and also the record of the prior strike case. The father had been mistaken about the number of years the DA offered. Perhaps Larry embellished the number to get his father to hire an attorney. The real offer was thirteen years in prison, still way too much. I met with the DA whom I had known for many years. I had been assigned with her in the mid-1980s to Central Trials. She was courteous, but had the reputation of being a tough criminal prosecutor. Before I was sufficiently prepared to negotiate with her, I mentioned I was not sure the prior arson strike was valid and that we needed to research it. A strict but honest DA, she said if the strike was not there, she would not proceed on it.

My client and two friends had come upon a house, with a wide-open back door, which they decided to burglarize. One remained outside as a lookout while the other two boys entered. They were part of a multi-ethnic criminal organization. One boy was Caucasian, one Hispanic, my client African American. While inside the house, Larry and the Caucasian boy began taking the victims' possessions. Larry found an empty backpack and loaded it with stolen goods. The friend put a folding knife he liked into his pocket. They rummaged through the victims' property with such zeal, they did not hear the warning from the lookout. They realized the victims had returned home while they were cleaning out the upstairs bedroom. They quickly ran into the bathroom and hid.

Upon entering the home, Mr. Longshore and his wife immediately knew there was a problem. They apprehensively climbed the stairs to the bedroom and noticed the closed bathroom door. Longshore opened the door and was accosted by the Caucasian boy wielding the knife. Longshore's hand was cut in the struggle. During the scuffle, my client escaped by pushing Longshore out of the way and running out of the house. The Caucasian boy ran out as well. The three boys ran at top speed past a neighborhood community center as Longshore chased after them. The groundskeeper recognized Larry and told him to slow down. A short time later, my client was arrested wearing the backpack. Both the victims and the groundskeeper identified Larry.

Larry had previously been convicted of setting fire to a condominium complex in violation of California Penal Code Section 451, commonly known as arson, a serious crime with potentially devastating consequences. If that fire had spread, many people might have died. Larry was charged with the prior arson strike, two counts of robbery, one count of burglary and aiding and abetting the assault with a deadly weapon. His case was grim.

After I learned the facts, I was sorry I had taken the case. I honestly believed I could not help him, but I had to try. I hired a defense psychiatrist to examine Larry. In the juvenile file, there was a mention by a previously appointed psychiatrist that Larry had a learning disability. I thought maybe I had an angle that the same problem causing the learning disability caused Larry's criminal inclinations. Perhaps I could garner some sympathy if I found a mental or emotional problem, a chemical imbalance in the brain that might mitigate his criminal intent. I sat with the DA and discussed the case. I told her that he had never been in jail before, despite his record. On the juvenile case, he had only been sentenced to home on probation. I noticed the DA's expression of surprise that he had been given probation on the prior since it was such a serious arson case.

To count as a juvenile strike prior, the law requires the prior fall within California Welfare and Institutions Code Section 707(b). In the juvenile case, Larry had been charged with two counts of arson, California Penal Code Sections 451(a) and 451(b), both expressly enumerated within California Welfare and Institutions Code Section 707(b). The juvenile file did not contain the final plea and sentence on the case. I petitioned and obtained a copy of the final disposition, which was a plea to Penal Code Section 451(c). The other two charges had been dropped. California Welfare and Institutions Code Section

707(b) is silent as to 451(c). Faithful to her word, the DA dismissed the prior strike. The offer changed from thirteen years in prison to five years.

Larry requested time to think about it and I wanted to finish the research on the case. The matter was continued one last time. While the Longshore case was pending and after I received the five year offer, the police crime lab completed a fingerprint analysis of a suspect who had burglarized a home and stolen a large screen TV, just two days before the Longshore robbery. When the neighbors watched the African American suspect with his Caucasian friend carrying the TV, they snapped a blurry photo of him. The fingerprint confirmed it was Larry. When I heard of the new filing, I was dismayed. I had won the battle, but it now seemed I would lose the war. When I had conveyed the new offer to the father, he was excited and thankful. Now I had to see him again to explain the offer was likely to change based on the new case against Larry.

Expecting the five-year offer to change, I met with the DA again. This time she told me Larry would now have to answer for this new charge by accepting her offer of five years on the original case and receive a concurrent sentence on the new case. I spoke with Larry, telling him this was now very serious and that not taking this deal would result in a massive amount of prison time. When we returned to court, Larry accepted the plea agreement. He will be out of prison before his twenty-third birthday, still a young man. Hopefully he can turn his life around.

* * * * * * * *

The good lawyer is not the man who has an eye to every side and angle of contingency, and qualifies all his qualifications, but who throws himself on your part so heartily, that he can get you out of a scrape.
— Ralph Waldo Emerson

Judge Walter Barber was as fine a man and judge as you would find on the Los Angeles County Superior Court. He had spent years presiding over juvenile cases at the courthouse. He respected me and added my name to the list of court-appointed attorneys. There were a lot of cases. I spent several years defending minors on cases ranging from drug and petty offenses to gang-related murders.

Most of my juvenile clients at the time were African American, a few Latino. There were some serious crimes, such as gang shootings. I handled a heartbreaking case where a remorseful, ten-year-old, shot and killed his best friend while playing with a gun. It was a tragic accident but the DA still charged him with manslaughter. Judge Barber would not let anything terrible happen to him. The minor would be placed in a foster home for some time. That was it. He was just too young for any real punishment.

Los Angeles is unusual in the sense that it has a "camp" system. When the punishment does not require a commitment to the Division of Juvenile Justice, state prison for juveniles, a minor might be sent to a probation camp. There are two such commitments, a short and long term camp. When a crime is not too serious, the minor could be sentenced to home on probation. At that time, a judge might sentence such a minor to a camp-stayed disposition. He would sentence him or her to camp, then "stay" the order, and the minor would go home on probation. If he or she did not do well, the minor would be sent to camp. This hammer over the minor's head was a way to keep him or her from breaking the law. I remember one boy whose mother worked at UCLA. One year she sent me tickets to a UCLA basketball game. Her son and some of his friends robbed a victim at a bus stop. Sentenced to a camp-stayed disposition, he ended up doing well, graduating from college. Judges do not use camp-stayed dispositions anymore.

There were crack cocaine cases, assaults, thefts, a variety of crimes. It was not lucrative, but was rewarding because I felt I was making a difference. Usually minors are scared, often from broken families, with no father. Many of these juveniles stayed in touch with me over the years. I would receive calls telling me they were in college or that they turned themselves around and they wanted to thank me.

I had one tragic case of a teenage girl who hid her pregnancy from her religious family. Because she was overweight, her pregnancy went unnoticed. Thinking the baby was born dead, she disposed of the body. Later, the body was found and traced to her. There was an autopsy and it was determined the baby had breathed. My client was charged with murder. It was horrible. An only child, she was a top student. The parents were overwhelmed with fear for their daughter. They never even knew she was pregnant. After a war with the DA's office, she was sentenced to a short-term camp commitment of sixty days.

Next to the courtroom there is a lockup where attorneys talk to their clients. Sometimes the court staff would offer me chocolate and I would ask if I could forego my piece and give it to my client. They would say, "Of course." On one case, police officers detained my sixteen-year-old client for a battery offense. They referred his case to the District Attorney's Office and Juvenile Probation Department. The case was filed and I was appointed to represent the minor. The matter resulted in an acquittal, due in part to some aggressive cross-examination of the arresting officer. Thinking the officer was angry at me, I hesitated when after the hearing, he asked for my business card.

Officer Simon James looked at me intently from across my desk as he outlined his problem. It had been a week since I reluctantly gave him my card. Apart from his job at the police department, James owned a private security company. There had been a shooting at a strip club in Hollywood. An unruly, armed and violent customer had to be dealt with by security personnel. James' security company was charged with minor licensing violations relating to the incident. The case had been pending in court nearly two years and James was unhappy with his lawyer. He wanted to hire me.

James' main competitor happened to be a high-ranking officer in the same police department. He owned a similar but smaller security company. Usually these businesses hire off duty police officers to provide security services. After the incident at the strip club, there was an unusually extensive investigation of James' company. He was charged with minor misdemeanor licensing violations, which if convicted, would have resulted in the loss of his job and security business. Suspicions about why so many resources were used for such a small violation fell on his competitor's relationship with the detectives.

I substituted in as attorney of record at "zero of ten" for trial. That means the trial would start within ten days. In order to persuade the judge to allow me on the case, I had to guarantee the court that I was ready for trial. I studied the newly acquired police reports and decided I would file a motion to dismiss based on a theory of "selective prosecution." I would subpoena the investigating detective and the owner of the rival security company to inquire about any undisclosed pressures put on the detective to find violations. A number of facts supported this argument. First, James had a thriving private security company. Second, the rival firm was smaller and not as successful. Third, the investigation used far more resources than the garden variety licensing violation. Fourth, the owner of the rival company very likely knew the detectives investigating James. Fifth, there had been a delay of about one year in the actual filing of the charges.

Driving back to my office from court, I was contemplating my argument for the selective prosecution motion. I had to file this motion as soon as possible, as the trial was just eight days away. The thick investigative reports were piled on the passenger seat of my car as I was driving sixty-five miles per hour on the freeway. It hit me like a ton of bricks: they waited too long to file the charges. I frantically started digging through the box of manila folders on my passenger seat to find the complaint. I could not believe my eyes. The allegation of the licensing violation on the date of the strip club shooting was filed one year and three days after the incident. The statute of limitations on misdemeanors in California is one year. I arrived at my office, immediately prepared a motion to dismiss based on a violation of the statute of limitations, drove back to the courthouse and filed it. Eight days later, the motion was heard and the case dismissed. In the two years the case had been pending, nobody had ever checked the date of the filing. Lawyers are hired to pay attention to details.

* * * * * * * *

Criminal defendants are not the only parties in court in need of representation. Sometimes witnesses require legal protection.

I was appointed to represent such a witness in 1989, to protect her Fifth Amendment rights on a notorious death penalty trial in Los Angeles called the "Night Stalker Case." From June 27, 1984 to August 8, 1985, a serial murderer terrorized the Los Angeles Basin. Usually he would strike at night. He targeted unsecured, freeway-close, yellow stucco homes to enter and burglarize, killing the occupants, often after sexually assaulting them. Satanic symbols, such as the downward pointing pentagram, were left at some crime scenes. Richard Ramirez was finally caught after a fingerprint revealed him to be the Night Stalker. Ramirez arrived at the downtown Los Angeles Greyhound Bus Station on August 29, 1985, after a visit in Arizona with his brother. Entering a corner grocery store, one of the owners recognized his photo, which that day had been plastered on the front page of all Los Angeles newspapers. The owner pointed at the killer, shouting, *"El Matador."* Ramirez ran two miles into East Los Angeles, jumping over fences through yards, searching for a car to steal. Three men heroically chased and restrained him until the police arrived. Ramirez was charged with fourteen murders and thirty-one other felonies.

My client was called to testify for the defense. She knew Ramirez, having burglarized homes with him during the day, while at the same time Ramirez was burglarizing and killing people at night. She testified Ramirez committed up to twenty-five nonviolent, daytime residential burglaries, using picks and pliers to gain entry. She was called by the defense to testify that, while Ramirez was a burglar, she never knew him to be a murderer and that violence was not a part of his method of operation. By the time she was called as a witness, the statute of limitations had expired on most of the burglaries they had committed together. She could not be prosecuted on those cases. The judge ruled that since she could not be prosecuted on the older cases, her Fifth Amendment protections did not apply. However, concerned about testimony leaking into burglaries done within the limitations period, the judge appointed me to protect her from potentially self-incriminating testimony.

In the end, her testimony damaged the defense. The District Attorney cross-examined her about the defendant's sloppiness during burglaries, consistent with the messy crime scenes of the "amateurish" Night Stalker. Richard Ramirez was found guilty of thirteen counts of murder, five attempted murders, eleven sexual assaults and fourteen burglaries. He is currently awaiting execution at San Quentin State Prison.

During a day off from trial, I visited several clients in the attorney visiting room at the Los Angeles County Jail. I sat on a circular wooden stool awaiting the arrival of my first client when a shackled Ramirez was brought into the attorney room and cuffed to a chair. He was facing me, peering right at me through the sunglasses he always wore. We stared at each other, neither showing any recognition of knowing the other. After about ten minutes, he nodded to me. I thought of his victims and the sheer terror they must have gone through. I did not acknowledge him.

Chapter IV

Adrenaline Overdose: DUI, Drugs & Domestic Violence

Anyway, no drug, not even alcohol, causes the fundamental ills of society. If we're looking for the source of our troubles, we shouldn't test people for drugs, we should test them for stupidity, ignorance, greed and love of power.
– P.J. O'Rourke

There are many types of illegal drugs. The state laws relating to drug crimes are found in the California Health and Safety Code. The laws distinguish among the classes of drugs, increasing the punishments for the more dangerous drugs. The California Health and Safety Code contains enhancement statutes when large quantities are at issue. These enhancements increase the punishment significantly.

During the night trial of Xavier Moore, I spent three weeks in day court, litigating a search and seizure motion on a huge cocaine bust. My client was Ignatius Thome. One of Thome's in-laws from Mexico was in the cocaine business. Ignatius was having financial difficulty and in return for money, agreed to store cocaine in his middle class home over the weekend. The authorities were surveilling the shipment and watched the boxes of cocaine delivered to the two-car garage. Search warrants were executed and the cocaine seized. My client never opened these boxes; nor did he have any intent to sell, only to warehouse the boxes for the weekend. Nonetheless, he was charged with conspiracy and possession for sale of massive amounts of cocaine. The punishment is very severe for possessing large quantities of cocaine, so settling this case was difficult. It did finally resolve with a prison term of five years, not the fifteen years the DA wanted. Ignatius was out in two and a half years.

Houses are built for people, farms for animals and crops. An unusual hybrid has emerged in recent years, houses with marijuana plants blossoming in every square foot. The house is gutted, no space for human habitation, just thousands of plants fed by sophisticated lighting and an entire cultivation system of watering and fertilizing. The houses have dark curtains or drapes obscuring the view inside from onlookers. Often an electrician would bypass the electrical lines from the street to hide evidence of the massive electricity usage. Sometimes electricity under-usage is a tip that marijuana cultivation is happening inside. The crime started out in Western Canada, in the Vancouver area and then moved southward throughout the United States like a wave. If you were to examine the history, you would see news stories, first from Canada, then Seattle, Northern California and down to San Diego. In addition to other ethnicities, two groups of Chinese were engaged in this enterprise: one Cantonese, one Fujianese. In each house, for a period of one year, three harvests of thousands of plants brought in millions of dollars. It was very profitable.

I represented a half dozen people prosecuted for these crimes in various courts throughout Central and Southern California. In each case, Federal Drug Enforcement agents investigated. Sometimes the cases were filed in California State Court, other times in Federal Court. A defendant is usually more fortunate to be tried in California courts, because state law generally has lower sentencing ranges than federal law. Sometimes authorities would obtain warrants to enter the house, secretly installing hidden cameras, catching the perpetrators on video. In other cases, they might only surveil the growers, following them from marijuana house to marijuana house, meeting to meeting, discovering co-conspirators in the process.

Since there was an abundance of evidence in these cases, most resolved without trial by pleas to minimal prison or jail terms. In many of the state cases, plea negotiations resulted in short sentences of ninety to one-hundred eighty days in jail for first offenders. The federal cases were more severe, usually resulting in prison terms from twenty-four months to ten years depending on the severity of the case, the criminal history of the defendant and the level of the participant's role in the crime.

* * * * * * * *

Drug sales and cultivation are felonies, whereas drug usage is misdemeanor conduct. Driving under the influence of drugs or alcohol is a common problem in our society, usually resulting in misdemeanor charges. One client, Timothy O'Malley, hired me twice to represent him on DUI charges.

Timothy is a tall, rugged man who managed a factory in Riverside. He was tough, a risk taker. He manufactured diversion safes, devices used for many years to protect valuables and important documents. During World War I, soldiers hid maps and codes in rifle ammunition. Today diversion safes, also called hidden safes, are commonly designed as everyday products, placed in plain view. The safes are cans of soda, cosmetics, cleaning products, books, any common household item. A thief would least expect to find jewelry in a food jar.

Timothy hired me after an arrest for driving under the influence. The case was prosecuted in Riverside Superior Court. I appeared at the arraignment and received the complaint and discovery, pleading the client not guilty. He was charged with two counts. Count One, a violation of California Vehicle Code Section 23152(a), prohibits driving under the influence of alcohol and/or drugs. Count Two, California Vehicle Code Section 23152(b), forbids driving with a blood alcohol level of .08 or above. Technically, one could be charged under 23152(a) with driving under the influence of alcohol, where the blood alcohol level is less than .08. Some drinkers are affected more by alcohol, or cannot tolerate even a small amount and are unable to drive safely with a low blood alcohol level. This tends to be rare and mostly applies to those with limited exposure to alcohol or who have allergies to it. Even if one can drive safely with a .08 blood alcohol level, it is a violation of the law.

Timothy needed my help to fight the charges. There are many defenses to a DUI charge. In Timothy's case, the police report indicated the time of arrest as approximately ten minutes before the breath-alcohol test. Timothy had been stopped just minutes after leaving his sister's home, located near the police station. It was not unreasonable that he could have arrived at the police station and taken the breath test within minutes of his arrest. Ten minutes was a stretch. The officer most likely erred in writing the time in his report, but it was not my job to correct him. My obligation was only to defend my client. Under the relevant California guidelines, the test operator must continuously observe the DUI suspect for a full fifteen minutes before the test is given to ensure the suspect does not eat, vomit or smoke, which might contaminate the breath sample.

Timothy rejected all plea bargains and demanded a trial. He had a relatively low blood alcohol level of .10. I advised Timothy that going to trial was expensive and risky. Under California law, a DUI conviction can result in a jail term for up to six months. When one goes to trial and loses, one forfeits the bargaining power to obtain a good plea agreement, ordinarily a period of probation, short-term alcohol school and a fine. One then risks being sentenced to jail. A judge might justify a jail sentence because after testimony, he or she believes the case is more serious or that the defendant perjured himself.

Timothy was a gambler, willing to risk his freedom. The DA was a new lawyer who would have been amenable to a plea bargain since the blood alcohol level was low, but would not dismiss the case. At trial, he threw in every argument he could, a mistake common to less experienced Deputy District Attorneys. Abraham Lincoln wrote in 1848: "In law it is good policy to never plead what you need not, lest you oblige yourself to prove what you cannot."

The DA called the officer who testified about my client's level of intoxication. The officer said he was driving unsafely. He related that Timothy had failed the field sobriety tests and that, in his opinion, was driving under the influence of alcohol.

On cross-examination, I asked the officer, "Did you write an arrest report in this matter?"

"I did."

"In training, were you taught the importance of writing an accurate report?"

"Of course."

"Did you write an accurate report in this case?"

"Certainly, I did."

"Do you wish to change anything in the report?"

"No."

Directing the officer's attention to the place in the report showing the time he stopped my client, I asked again if he wished to change anything. He said no. I then took out the breath test printout and showed the officer that the test was only ten minutes after the initial stop. The officer became extremely nervous, realizing my strategy. It was too late. He was stuck. He had already testified he had reviewed his report and it was accurate. I then went to the place in the police report where the officer signed that he followed the requirements for administering the breath test, including observing the suspect for fifteen minutes prior to taking the test. "You checked the box, which indicated that you observed the suspect for a full fifteen minutes before administering the intoxilyzer test?" He said that he had. "But, Officer, you only stopped him ten minutes prior to the test," I argued. "It is not possible that you observed the suspect for five minutes before you met him, correct?"

Timothy took the stand and told his story. He was at his sister's house for her birthday. Though he did not ordinarily drink, he toasted his sister just before he left. Within a minute, he was stopped by police and ten minutes later given a breath test. I asked Timothy what he did for a living. It was not relevant to the DUI charge, but the DA did not object. Timothy talked about the safes he makes. I brought out a couple of these deception safes, handing a Pledge can to Timothy, who showed the jury how one could unscrew the bottom and place valuables inside. He said he had regular meetings with local police departments to market his products in order to stop thefts. The jury was fascinated.

During the prosecutor's cross-examination, Timothy handled himself well. The defense rested. In closing argument, the DA brought out three large bottles of water. He told the jury this was the quantity of alcohol Timothy must have consumed within an hour in order to get his blood alcohol level to .10. The DA missed a great opportunity to improvise an argument that Timothy's defense was just like his safes, a deception.

During my closing argument, I held up the bottles, arguing this was a great amount of liquid. I said, "There is a missing piece in this trial. The arresting officer should have testified Mr. O'Malley desperately complained he had to go to the bathroom. One cannot drink this much liquid and not have to use a toilet. Police officers know this and always record in their reports the suspect's need to urinate. It is great evidence that a suspect drank too much. This evidence is missing because Mr. O'Malley did not drink alcohol, or any other liquid, to excess." The jury found Timothy not guilty. About three years later, Timothy called me. With a sheepish tone, he told me about a second DUI arrest. Here we go again.

* * * * * * * *

A driver suspected of DUI must submit to a breath or blood test. Urine tests were previously utilized but due to the high error factor, have been discontinued. Timothy had a .14 blood alcohol level in his urine. This time around, I suggested Timothy accept a plea bargain. I thought the judge might punish him if he went to trial and lost because he had a prior DUI arrest, even though he was acquitted. I feared a likely jail sentence after trial; Timothy was unafraid. We started trial.

My intended defense was based on the inherent error factor in urine tests. There were no problems with the police report, and unlike in the previous case, the judge was strict. I quoted the National Traffic Safety Board, which recommended abolishing urine as a form of DUI test because of the high error factor. I discussed the inaccuracy of urine testing in my opening statement. Then the officer was called to the stand and testified to Timothy's bad driving, poor performance on the field sobriety tests, odor of alcohol, unsteady gait, bloodshot eyes and slurred speech.

In my cross-examination, I asked the officer if she was aware the urine test was the least accurate method to determine one's blood alcohol level. She said it was an approved test. A lucky break occurred during the questioning of the officer about the evidence envelope containing Timothy's urine sample. On direct examination, she was about to open the envelope when I asked the judge if I could take the witness on *voir dire*. This meant to question the witness about what she expected to find inside the envelope. The judge allowed it. I asked her, "You are about to open a sealed envelope. Did *you* seal that envelope?"

"Yes."

"What did you put inside?"

"I placed a small jar containing the defendant's urine sample inside."

"What does that jar look like?" She described its basic dimensions and then said there was a label on the jar where she wrote the defendant's name and case number, which she said was her customary practice. I asked her only a few more questions. The officer opened the envelope, and much as she described, there was a jar with a cap and liquid inside. The DA asked if this was the jar containing Mr. O'Malley's urine sample and the officer replied affirmatively. The DA finished her questioning. I asked the judge for permission to approach the witness. I held up the jar, looking at it. "I'm holding the jar which you just testified Mr. O'Malley handed you. You then sealed it. Is that correct?"

"Yes."

"You testified you secured a label on the jar with Mr. O'Malley's name and case number." As I put the jar in front of her, I questioned, "Can you tell me where his name appears?" Dumbfounded, she looked at the blank label. "As you look at the jar, can you tell me where the case number is written?" No answer, quiet. Nothing was written on it. "Officer, you just testified you had written Mr. O'Malley's name and case number on the label." No response. "This is the wrong jar; isn't that correct, Officer?"

"Maybe I was wrong and did not write the name and the case number."

"You were not wrong, Officer. You just testified under penalty of perjury that you had written the name and case number. You also testified that it is your customary practice to do so. Isn't that true?"

"Yes, it is."

"This is the wrong jar. You tested the wrong jar?"

"You might be correct."

I did not call Timothy to testify. I felt we already had a strong position. After the DA finished her case, we rested on the "insufficient state of the evidence." In closing, I argued the entire time that the jury must only convict those who are shown to be guilty beyond a reasonable doubt. One of our fundamental rights is the presumption of innocence until *proven* guilty. I argued that the DA failed. "We do not know Mr. O'Malley's actual blood alcohol level. The DA's office does not know it. You do not know it."

Since the officer testified Timothy failed the field sobriety tests, drove poorly and showed objective symptoms of intoxication, the jury did have some evidence to believe Timothy was driving under the influence. The jury hung, eight for not guilty, four for guilty. In a misdemeanor case, often the courts will not allow a retrial, especially where a jury hangs in favor of the defendant. Declaring a mistrial, the judge dismissed the case. Timothy won again.

* * * * * * * *

Misty Ling Wan was raised with the imperative that, like her mother, she would someday become a nurse. Mother and father had met working in the operating room at the Beijing Peoples' First Hospital, where dad was a cardiac surgeon and mom a head nurse. Misty was proud of her parents and dedicated herself to her studies. She worked hard in school and in her profession. Earning her nursing degree from a first-rate nursing college in New York, she had done well in the university back in her hometown, Tianjin, a large port city on China's northeast coast, about an hour's drive from Beijing. After college, she applied for and was accepted into nursing school. She studied diligently, graduating with honors.

Nurse Wan began her career in the emergency room at Santa Monica Hospital. She loved and excelled at her job. At first, working long hours, she did not have the social life befitting a pretty, single woman. Many potential suitors from the ranks of her coworkers chased her. Wisely, she was careful not to mix work with pleasure. After a time, she met and began to date Adam Lisban, an up and coming Los Angeles stock broker, whose office was located in a classy downtown skyscraper.

Adam invited Misty to the brokerage firm's annual Christmas party at the corporate headquarters downtown. They looked forward to the party and arrived on time bringing gifts and wearing party attire. Misty's cheerful green dress caught many admiring eyes. There was a generous buffet of appealing and expensive foods, and a full cocktail bar. Misty enjoyed the food but stayed away from the bar, instead drinking non-alcoholic punch she poured into her glass from a large crystal punchbowl. Adam spent a little too much time at the bar. When they left, both suspected Adam should not drive. Misty felt happy and energetic, "Hey, I feel great, I'm not tired at all. Let me drive." Fortunately for Misty, Adam overruled her.

On the way home, Adam was stopped by California Highway Patrol officers who observed Adam's BMW weaving. He was ordered out of the car and required to perform field sobriety tests, which he failed. Upon his arrest, officers engaged Misty in a conversation intended to determine if she was capable of driving the vehicle home, or if she too was intoxicated. What the officers discovered shocked both Adam and Misty. Misty was displaying symptoms of amphetamine intoxication. To Misty, this was impossible. She neither drank nor took drugs. Yet the officers recorded a pulse rate of 128 beats per minute, "extremely" dilated pupils slow to react to light, flushed face and poor performance on standardized field sobriety tests. Misty was arrested for a violation of Health and Safety Code, Section 11550(a), a misdemeanor commonly called "being under the influence of a controlled substance." She was handcuffed, taken to jail, escorted to the bathroom and handed a jar for urine collection. Several weeks later, the Los Angeles County Sheriff's Crime Lab tested the urine sample and determined it positive for ecstasy, an illegal synthetic drug with hallucinogenic and amphetamine-like properties, often called the "club drug" due to its common use at nightclubs and parties.

Two days after her arrest and one day after the posting of her bail, Misty appeared in my office. She was insistent she was drug free. "There is no way that urine test will come back positive," she said. "I don't take drugs. As a registered nurse, I would lose my license." Misty's second point was right: she would lose her license should she be convicted of a drug offense. Unfortunately, she was not so correct about the first point. She was in fact under the influence of ecstasy. Both the Los Angeles County Sheriff's Department Crime Lab and two independent labs I hired confirmed that very unfortunate fact.

California Health and Safety Code Section 11550(a) imposes a mandatory minimum jail term of 90 days as a consequence of suffering such a conviction, in addition to three years of probation. One of the probationary terms requires a probationer not possess or be present in any place where narcotics are used, a difficult predicament for a nurse who spends most of her time in an emergency room. Fortunately for most first time drug abusers, California Penal Code Section 1000 allows first offenders to participate in a Deferred Entry of Judgment (DEJ) program. Under this law, the defendant enters a plea of guilty to the charge early in the proceedings. The court accepts the plea but does not sentence the defendant. Instead, the defendant attends six months of drug classes and stays out of trouble for eighteen to twenty-four months. If the defendant fails the program, he will be sentenced up to the maximum period allowed by the statute for which he was convicted. If the defendant satisfactorily completes the program, the case will be dismissed and the defendant will never have been sentenced. Since under California law, a conviction does not occur until one is sentenced, the defendant has not been convicted of a crime. The problem with this procedure is that state licensing authorities such as the Nursing Board consider the plea of guilty, even if only for DEJ purposes, sufficient grounds to take punitive action. Any way you looked at it, Nurse Wan's license was in jeopardy, and she had no choice but to push for trial.

Having been a prosecutor, I knew the least likely way to get the DA to dismiss this charge was to argue Misty was unaware she ingested the ecstasy. She was a young pretty professional, wearing a party dress, having just left a late night affair at a posh upper class brokerage firm's headquarters. To the DA, this was just another fancy Hollywood type partying with her rich drunk boyfriend driving dangerously in his showy BMW. As expected, my pleas fell on deaf ears as I tried over and over to convince the courtroom DA to dismiss the allegation. I made an appointment with the Deputy DA in charge of the courthouse, and was rudely told to "tell it to the jury." "Fine," I said, "set the case for trial." Of course, Misty's situation was not helped by the fact that her boyfriend was also fighting the charge. He had a blood alcohol level above the legal limit, but only by a few points, and was represented by a self-important Century City lawyer.

The day of trial arrived. I brought several character witnesses, ready to testify about Misty's impeccable reputation for honesty, and the fact that she did not take drugs. I also had one potential witness from the party who "heard" the punch "might" have been spiked. There was no way the judge was going to allow this hearsay and speculation, but maybe it would help with the DA. Several trial prosecutors, waiting to be sent out to trial, were in the master calendar courtroom. My case was yet to be assigned to a trial DA. It was a relatively small case, a misdemeanor in a sea of felonies. I saw DA William Katz, my former supervisor from CT 13, in the courtroom and greeted him, exchanging pleasantries. He was waiting to get sent out to trial on a murder case, and asked what I had. I told him about my ridiculous case, never for a second thinking he could or would help. I told him that the office policy had changed and that when we worked together years ago, we would never file on the passenger in such situations. He looked at the DA's file and asked, "Do you think your client can convince her boyfriend to plead to the DUI. If so, I will dismiss the case against her. I mentioned William's proposal to Misty. Without missing a beat, Misty grabbed her boyfriend's hand tugging him out of the courtroom. Twenty minutes later, a defeated Adam Lisban re-entered the courtroom and pleaded no contest to the DUI. Misty's case was dismissed.

* * * * * * * *

There are thirty-six state and eleven federal prisons in California. Half the state prisons are situated in the middle of California, a stone's throw from Interstate 5. It was on this freeway that Randi Phu travelled from her home in the San Gabriel Valley to Corcoran State prison. Built on what was once Tulare Lake, home of the Tachi Indians, Corcoran State Prison lies three and a half hours north of Los Angeles by car. She arrived in time for her scheduled visit with handsome boyfriend, Angel Barrera. Angel was doing time for a robbery committed at a San Bernardino convenience store. He was positively identified when the store clerk recognized Angel's bicep tattoo *Suzy*, the name of Angel's former girlfriend. *Suzy* was found in a police computer data bank, searchable using a suspect's distinctive features. Maybe next time the genius commits a robbery, he should just tattoo his home address on his forehead and save everybody the trouble. Born in the city formerly known as Saigon, twenty-five-year old Randi Phu was short, overweight, plain-looking and noticeably insecure. She had met Angel and began to date him a little over a year prior to his arrest. This wasn't Randi's first visit to the prison, and it wasn't the first time she brought him narcotics.

While her parents counseled against this relationship, Angel was Randi's first long-term boyfriend and she was especially fond of him. The fact that he was incarcerated enhanced Randi's passion for him; her worry, anxiety and longing grew as each day passed. She often wrote that she missed him dearly and, of course, would wait for him. At first, Angel's letters expressed his strong feelings of love and his yearning to be with her. He urged her to visit often. After a year of love letters, his tone began to change. He started to write of his fears of the other inmates, and that he could avoid physical harm by supplying the other prisoners with drugs. He told of threats against his life. Angel's letters played to Randi's fears, and she began to plan how she would help him. It wasn't until after her arrest that Randi learned of the outside network Angel had set up to receive payments for the anticipated sales of the dope.

Losing one's freedom is not the only consequence of a prison commitment. Once sentenced to incarceration, an inmate loses his privacy. Officers were intercepting Angel's correspondence and knew of Randi's plans. They also monitored and recorded the occasional phone call Angel was permitted. The silly encoded conversations told of the date and time the product would be delivered and evidenced Randi's feeble attempts to conceal the scheme. Transporting heroin hidden under a bandage fastened to her hip, Randi was arrested entering the prison.

It is a well-known fact among lawyers that prosecutorial policies tend to reflect the political nature of the jury pool in the local community. A tough-on-crime community will fill jury boxes with jurors more likely to convict, while moderate communities will send jurors who might not be so inclined. It is almost always better to try a case before a Santa Monica jury than one impaneled in Simi Valley. The corridor housing central California's Interstate 5 freeway is filled with communities largely inhabited by prison officials or workers having something to do the corrections industry. In other words, the jury pool for the Superior Court in Corcoran California was filled with potential jurors who either worked at a state prison, had a loved one who did, or who earned a living in an industry that somehow supported the prison system.

Randi was charged with crimes occurring during two visits: two counts of Possession of Narcotics on Prison Grounds in violation of California Penal Code, Section 4573.6; two counts of Possession of Narcotics with Intent to Disperse on Prison Grounds in violation of California Penal Code, Section 4573.9; and Conspiracy under Penal Code Section 182. Having posted the $180,000 bond for his daughter, Randi's irate father brought her to my office. I had represented Randi's brother on a minor criminal matter several years earlier and had worked out a deal avoiding a conviction. At the time, father and son were pleased with the outcome. On this day, father and daughter were anything but pleased. Both angry and tearful, their screaming voices were like daggers thrown into each other's hearts. I told them both to settle down. "We have a bigger problem here than your emotions." Randi had committed a crime the state legislature viewed as very serious and required a potentially lengthy period of incarceration. In addition, we faced an extremely conservative jury venire, a tough prosecutor, and a container-load of evidence including the heroin, letters in Randi's handwriting and likely recordings of their conversations. This was truly a nightmare.

After a three and a half hour drive, we appeared for the arraignment in Kings County Superior Court, Corcoran

Division. Upon arrival, the DA immediately requested Randi be taken into custody arguing that, even though she was a US Citizen, he feared Randi would flee to her country of birth, Vietnam. I had come armed with Randi's passport just in case something like this happened. I offered it up to the judge in lieu of increasing the already high bail. Randi and Angel were named in the same complaint; Angel was charged with conspiracy and a host of prior prison commitments, potentially adding years to his sentence. Randi was facing a maximum of eight years in prison, Angel ten years. Randi glanced lovingly at Angel throughout the arraignment, while Randi's dad peered hatefully at him. Dad and I spent the month before the arraignment explaining to Randi that Angel was, in fact, no angel at all, and had used her love and affection as a tool to recruit her to commit a serious crime for Angel's benefit. "He jeopardized your freedom and safety by using you to advance his criminal agenda. What would you get from the heroin? Nothing. His small income from selling heroin was more important than the risk of your rotting in prison. You don't matter to him." Randi didn't care; she loved him and that was it.

Over the next three months, we returned regularly to the court for pretrial hearings. Each time I would receive new batches of reports. There were recorded and transcribed telephone conversations between the defendants, photographs of the heroin affixed to Randi's hip, lab reports, copies of letters from Randi and letters from Angel, read by prison officials even before posting in the US mail. With no feasible defense and facing a trial in California's prison heartland, Randi was forced into a plea deal. The DA agreed to dismiss the more serious charges of possession with intent to disperse and conspiracy in exchange for a guilty plea to one straight possession charge.

Randi received a sentence of two years in the state prison and was released for good behavior after serving one year, half her sentence.

* * * * * * * *

Strange is our situation here upon earth. Each of us comes for a short visit, not knowing why, yet sometimes seeming to a divine purpose. From the standpoint of daily life, however, there is one thing we do know: that we are here for the sake of others.
– Albert Einstein

As time goes on, an attorney develops a large network of potential clients. A friend in trouble will call. The friend becomes the client. The client, who has been represented by the attorney for years, becomes the friend. Friends and clients merge. The lawyer learns whether one is a good person and does not judge based on allegations, but instead on his own perception of the client's character.

In addition to my criminal cases, my law partner, Jeff, was doing business and civil cases. We became acquainted with many businessmen. Jacob Rubin was an Israeli businessman who owned an electronics company. Jeff represented him on transactional matters such as contracts and business filings and also on litigation cases. Jacob would often call us with questions. Sometimes he would call late at night asking me to join him at a fancy Westside restaurant for a meeting with a potential business partner or early in the morning inquiring about negotiating benefits for a new lease. He became our good friend. He liked having us around because we could answer his legal questions and we enjoyed his company. Though he lived in the United States for many years, he remained active in Israeli politics. Jacob was well known in the Israeli community in America and would refer us other Israeli clients. His knowledge about Israeli politics seemed limitless. Jacob invited Jeff and me to a fundraiser for Israel. He said to be ready for a limousine to pick us up that evening. The limo arrived at 7 p.m. and drove us to a lavish Beverly Hills home. We walked to the front door and knocked. Incredibly, the man answering the door was Ariel Sharon, the former Defense Minister and future Prime Minister of Israel. We chatted for half an hour when Jacob walked up and said, "Ariel, I see you met my lawyers, Sandy and Jeff." That was in 1996. In 1998, Jacob invited Jeff and me to the 50th Anniversary of Israel's Independence Celebration at the Biltmore Hotel. Jeff and I arrived and sat at the table Jacob had reserved. There was seating for ten but only eight guests were there, including us. We introduced ourselves and started talking. We did not see Jacob who, in typical fashion, was late. After an hour, Jacob and a guest approached us. "Ariel, you remember my lawyers, Sandy and Jeff?" "Yes," he said, shaking our hands, "I remember you, hello."

In another limousine ride, Jacob took Jeff and me to a small lunch gathering to meet a well-known senator from Delaware, Joe Biden, now United States Vice-President. Biden was speaking mostly about Israel, as this was a group of Israel supporters. It was an intimate crowd of about twenty. We sat around and talked, listening to Biden. There were times we broke into small groups, and at one point, just Jeff and I were talking to him. Because Senator Biden was on the Senate Judiciary Committee, I told him I thought the federal sentencing guidelines were overly harsh, giving too much power to the U.S. Attorney's Office and not enough discretion to federal judges. Biden was diplomatic, agreeing judicial discretion is important, but there was an effort in the Senate to ensure people were treated equally under the law, thus requiring mandatory standardized sentencing. Many years later I was proven correct. In the case of the *United States of America vs. Booker,* the Supreme Court ruled that mandatory sentencing guidelines are unconstitutional. The remedy was to keep the guidelines as advisory.

I am continually struck by our connectivity, how one person leads me to another, how a previous case leads to a new one. A play, *Six Degrees of Separation*, proposes that everyone in the world is connected by no more than six degrees of acquaintances. I am one degree connected to Vice-President Biden, two degrees from President Obama. Since I once met Ted Kennedy, I am two degrees of separation from John F. Kennedy and more provocatively, if the President introduced his little brother, two degrees from Marilyn Monroe.

* * * * * * *

Jealousy is a tiger that tears not only its prey, but also its own raging heart.
– Chinese proverb

Criminal defense attorneys are always on call. Clients are arrested twenty-four hours a day. Law enforcement officers are in the same position, especially detectives who must be ready to respond to a crime scene at any hour, day or night.

In a small city in Orange County, a hard-working Sheriff's detective, Clark Riley, married an extremely jealous woman, especially envious of his long hours. The couple constantly argued, she often accusing him of cheating. She would threaten that if she caught him with another woman, she would ruin his career and life. After several months of bitter arguing, she went to the local police department and filed a report alleging her husband had beaten her. She reported that he punched her face and head between fifteen and twenty times. The officer taking the statement recorded the woman on videotape.

Detective Riley was arrested, hired an attorney and appeared in court. Soon it became obvious attorney and client had divergent attitudes as to how the case should be handled. Extremely frustrated, Riley sought a second opinion and complained to his good friend, Officer Simon James, who sent him to me. Riley told me about his case and that he was due in court on Friday before Judge Theodore Sullivan. I responded in surprise, "Teddy Sullivan is a judge now!" I was genuinely happy for Teddy. During law school, I spent a semester as a law clerk at the Los Angeles County Public Defender's Office, Juvenile Division. My supervisor was a young Deputy Public Defender named Teddy Sullivan. Teddy and I became friends although I had not seen him in many years. I had no idea he was appointed to the Bench. Detective Riley hired me.

A plea bargain in this case was out of the question. My client would lose his job if he pleaded guilty to anything. The case resulted in a jury trial. The victim testified that my client, when confronted with his cheating, had pummeled her face and head repeatedly. As well as exposing her jealous character, cross-examination revealed she had never seen a doctor for treatment of the fifteen to twenty fist blows. The next witness was the officer who had taken the victim's statement. The videotape showed her comfortably talking to the police just minutes after the assault allegedly took place. It showed the victim touching places on her face and head where she allegedly felt pain. The way she touched herself was peculiar. She was pushing hard to see where there might be pain. I showed this videotape to the jury while I cross-examined the officer. I stopped the tape at every point she pressed at her face and head, and asked the officer, "When you saw her touching herself here, did she wince in pain?" Of course, I already knew the answer. Everybody in the courtroom was watching the same videotape, saw the same thing, everybody except this officer. Strangely, he said, "Yes." On the videotape, her face was perfectly still as she touched and pushed at it. The whole jury could observe this. I stopped the videotape at least ten times. She did not once make any facial gestures of pain, but each time the officer said she was grimacing in pain as she patted her face. I looked at the jury. Their expressions revealed disbelief. I provoked the officer as much as possible on the issue. The jury knew the officer was lying. They were watching him lie. I called friends of the couple to the witness stand. They testified to the wife's jealous behavior, starting fights, slapping the husband in public and threatening him. He would never touch her. The jury returned a verdict of not guilty.

* * * * * * * *

A strange roommate arrangement resulted in an allegation of domestic violence against a Korean client. A married couple lived in a two-bedroom apartment, one bedroom occupied by a male roommate. The wife had begun a secret relationship with this roommate. As the affair progressed, the husband naturally discovered it. The husband learned the roommate had given the wife a ring, hoping the wife would divorce her husband and marry him. Making matters worse, the wife accused the husband of spousal abuse. At the police station, she showed the officers red marks on her face "where my husband beat me." The police arrested him and he hired me. The DA wanted jail time, while

I insisted the case be dismissed. A jury trial ensued and the DA called his first witness, the victim. She testified about what my client had allegedly done to her. On cross-examination I asked, "Are you having an affair with the roommate?"

"No."

"Are you trying to get rid of your husband because you want to marry your roommate?"

"No."

"Your roommate is here today and I've talked to him. We know about the ring he gave you. Tell us what the ring was for?" She broke down. She had no idea that we knew about the ring. She could not stop crying. "The roommate gave you the ring, because he wanted to marry you, didn't he?" She did not answer. "And you accepted that ring, didn't you?" She was silent. "I have no further questions of this witness, your Honor." My client was acquitted.

In another unusual roommate situation, a rookie DA handed me a victory. Eve Chang owned a condominium, lived in one of the rooms and rented the remaining rooms to two men. One man, Dustin Tran, had lived there for some time, while the other, my client, Hong Lin, only one month. Dustin was an obnoxious and irresponsible tenant, usually late on his rent. He touched women visitors inappropriately causing Ms. Chang and her friends to fear him. Late one night, reeking of alcohol and screaming about ants in his room, Dustin confronted Ms. Chang. She entered the room, and seeing no ants, walked back to the living room where Dustin continued berating her. My client, Mr. Lin, having heard the commotion, awoke, entered the living room and escorted Dustin back to his room. The next day, Dustin went to work, his face beaten and bruised. He worked all day and at 7:00 p.m. went to the police station to report that my client had attacked him. This was roughly twenty hours after the incident. He told the police that my client had battered him with his hands and fists. He said he tried to fight back but that my client won the fight and left him injured. Then, Dustin told the police, he went back to his room, closed the door and went to bed.

Four days later a detective showed up at the home. All three were there: the landlady, Ms. Chang; my client, Mr. Lin; and the "victim," Dustin Tran. The detective spoke to the victim privately. He showed the detective the plastic storage bins with metal brackets the defendant "used to hit me in the face while inside my bedroom." This statement was in complete contradiction to his earlier statement that he was fist fighting with my client in the living room, turned around after the fight, went to his bedroom, closed the door and went to sleep.

Mr. Lin was charged with battery. I talked to the Head DA, my former officemate, Sarah Levine. I asked her on which of the two statements she would proceed. They were so different. It was obvious he was lying. I told the DA that I had a witness, Ms. Chang, the landlady, who said the victim was drunk and my client had only stopped the man from harassing her and escorted him to his room. Once in his room, the victim started throwing things around, including breaking apart the stackable storage bins. He was angry, violent, inebriated and unsteady on his feet. He was throwing things out of his room into the area where the landlady and my client were standing. When he would throw metal objects, he would fall.

Sarah said, "Look at the photographs. See how beaten this man's face appears." I said I knew the photos looked bad, but both my client and the landlady maintained that my client never touched him. This guy was just going crazy. The DA would neither dismiss the case nor would she reduce the charge.

She recognized the problems, but the injuries to the victim were so bad, she simply could not resolve the case.

The trial started and we began picking the jury. One of the jurors was a victim of domestic violence. I thought she would either see through the victim's lies, or be reminded of how she was beaten and find the defendant guilty for spite. I spent a lot of time with her in *voir dire* talking about the case. I told her that she could not confuse what happened to her with this case. She satisfied me that she would not allow herself to be biased. John Bauman, my former DA supervisor in West Covina, taught me it is always wise to challenge and remove a potential problem juror during *voir dire*. He said you are usually sorry if you don't. John was right.

The victim took the witness stand and told a third story, completely different from the first two. I impeached him with the first, then the second. I took apart his third story. I asked him specifically what he did the next morning after the purported beating. He awoke and saw how black and blue he was, but went to work anyway. I asked if he stopped anywhere before he went to work. He said he went straight to work, stayed all day and did not leave until the workday ended at 7:00 p.m., when he drove to the police station. He arrived at the police department at 7:20. I pointed out that his face was battered and asked why he decided not to go to a doctor. He said he did go to the doctor. I asked him when he had time. "You testified you went directly from home to work and directly from work to the police. Then you testified you went directly home. You never said, 'I went to the doctor.'"

"I went to the doctor."

"When did you go to the doctor?"

"I went in the morning."

"Didn't you just tell the jury you went directly to work in the morning?"

"Oh, I went after work."

"I'm holding the police report and it shows you arrived at 7:20. You already testified you went straight to the police station after you left work at 7:00."

In the police report, he indicated he had not sought medical help nor did he plan to. He was caught in multiple lies. I called Ms. Chang to the witness stand. She testified Tran belligerently accosted her about the ants. Seeing no ants, she exited the room. He continued yelling as he followed her into the hallway. She told him it was too late to do anything about it, that she would call pest control in the morning. Unsatisfied, Tran remained verbally abusive. Ms. Chang testified that my client came out of his room to calm the man down. My client escorted him to his room. "Take it easy and go to sleep." The drunken victim went even more ballistic and started throwing things. He stumbled and fell a couple of times. Ms. Chang said she was not aware how he became injured. She was present the entire time and Mr. Lin never touched him.

On cross-examination, the inexperienced DA asked all the wrong questions. Every young lawyer is taught never to ask a question for which he or she does not already know the answer. For most lawyers, this is a difficult rule to follow. You are cross-examining a witness, making great progress toward your defense. You have the witness just where you want him, then blow it because you ask one question too many, and it destroys your defense. Consider the following scenario. The client is charged with mayhem, specifically biting off the victim's ear. The prosecution witness is on the stand and the lawyer is cross-examining him.

Q: So, is it fair to say you did not see my client's face near the victim's head?

A: Correct.

Q: And you did not see my client's mouth approaching the victim's ear?

A: Yes.

Q: And you did not see my client's teeth encircling the victim's ear?

A: Correct.

Q: And you did not see my client's teeth bite down on the victim's ear.

A: That's correct.

Q. Anyway, you did not see the victim cry in agony as his ear was being bitten off?

A. Right.

(This is where the lawyer should stop and sit down. Instead, the young lawyer just cannot help himself.)

Q: Then how do you know my client bit off the victim's ear?

A: Because I saw him spit it out.

Another funny example of asking one question too many involves a rookie police officer testifying about a defendant's level of intoxication. The enthusiastic defense attorney asks, "You have been an officer for just three months, correct?"

"Yes."

"And you have conducted only two DUI investigations?"

"That's correct."

"And based on that meager training, you concluded the defendant was driving under the influence of alcohol?"

"No."

"No? Then on what basis did you form the opinion he was under the influence?"

"My twenty-five years as a bartender."

The DA unskillfully asked Ms. Chang a question that arguably related to the victim's character. He opened the floodgates. She told the jury how the victim had threatened to burn her house down, how he sometimes did not pay her and how she was afraid to evict him. She told of the victim's drunkenness and abuse of women who came to visit her. It was obvious I was winning the case. I decided not to put my client on the stand.

The jury went out and a note was sent to the judge. Several jurors indicated that the split was eleven to one and that the foreperson was the holdout and would not do her job to alert the judge of the deadlock. The foreperson was the lady I spent so much time with, the one who promised not to allow her victimhood get in the way of being fair. The judge asked the jurors to deliberate longer to reach a verdict. There was now a heated argument emanating from the jury room. Multiple notes came back to the judge from different jurors. It was hopeless. The judge again brought them out and asked how they were now split. They said, "Eleven to one for not guilty." The judge dismissed the case.

Chapter V

Human Vice: Slavery, Trafficking & Sex Workers

In high profile cases, the media tends to frame stories in the context of good versus evil, often failing to acknowledge the nuances of the events. This happened in the disturbing and famous "Thai Slavery Case" I handled in the United States District Court. Investigators found scores of illegal Thai workers in a two-story, barbed-wired, seven-unit apartment complex in a Los Angeles suburb. The sun had yet to rise on this 1995 August morning, when federal, state and local law enforcement agents forced open the compound's spiked gates, waking the undocumented workers sprawled on crowded floors. The laborers were transported to detention facilities in Los Angeles, then questioned and released.

I was contacted by a group of Thai immigrants referred to my law firm by Ted Sarkisian, the DA from the Maestro of Break Dance Case, then working at an international law firm in Thailand. There were six defendants. My job was to represent one of the defendants and hire counsel for three others. The defendants were accused of, among other charges, holding these

Thai workers in involuntary servitude, a serious federal offense. The FBI reports and the discovery were voluminous.

The defendants were manufacturing garments for well-known fashion companies. According to the media, the objective was to profit from sales of clothing using sweatshop labor performed by a captive work force. The workers were poor Thai women with little education. The defendants were accused of fraudulently misleading the laborers who entered the U.S. after receiving phony visas and passports. A sham tour company would transport the workers from the airport to the apartment compound. Allegedly, they were deceived about the nature of their work, the wages and the severe restrictions on their freedom. The defendants purportedly intended to confiscate the workers' travel documents and restrict free communication with their families. According to law enforcement reports, the workers, subjected to an unlawful debt, were held as virtual slaves in the compound.

My client began as a worker, eventually marrying one of the other defendants. She changed her status from worker to manager. Her nuanced story cannot be viewed simply as "good versus evil" and is reminiscent of the 1975 Patty Hearst Case. Patty Hearst, granddaughter of San Francisco millionaire William Randolph Hearst, was a student at the University of California, Berkeley. On February 4, 1974, she was abducted from her apartment by armed members of the Symbionese Liberation Army. Two months later, she joined the SLA as "Tania," the name of Che Guevara's wife. Shortly after, she was caught on camera wielding a gun during a Hibernia Bank robbery in San Francisco and firing an automatic weapon from the back of a truck during the robbery of Mel's Sporting Goods in Los Angeles. Arrested in San Francisco on September 18, 1975, she was charged with armed robbery.

Hearst's defense, led by attorney F. Lee Bailey, argued that like a captive "prisoner of war," she had been brainwashed and was not capable of making a rational decision. Patty Hearst had been confined in a small closet for two months before she transformed into an SLA terrorist. Her initial sentence of thirty-five years was reduced to seven years and later commuted by President Carter after she spent twenty-two months in prison. President Clinton pardoned her in 2001. I would argue a similar defense for my client in the Thai Slavery Case.

Many workers gave statements against my client, alleging she operated a commissary from 1994 to 1995, where she offered food and goods at inflated prices. Further, my client, along with the other defendants, was charged with threatening physical harm to a worker and her family in Thailand, should she attempt to escape. The indictment alleged she willfully participated in the transportation of a laborer from Thailand to the United States, "unlawfully inveigling, decoying, seizing, confining, kidnapping and abducting the worker."

The subtleties of the case became more evident as the defendants' version of the facts became known. The defendants had taken the workers to the doctor if sick, to the grocery store for food and supplies, and to Las Vegas for vacation. There were photographs of parties in Las Vegas where the workers and defendants were having fun, laughing and joking, workers feeding cake to one of the guards.

Ultimately the defendants accepted a plea bargain. The case received such extensive media coverage, the United States Attorney advised that the plea bargain had to be decided at the Justice Department in Washington, D.C. My client was facing twenty years if convicted at trial. Fortunately for her, the plea agreement concluded with a forty-eight month prison term. The case was over, yet the story lingered for many years. I later learned that an exhibit memorializing this event was designed at the Smithsonian Institute in Washington, D.C.

* * * * * * *

In another human trafficking case, Ms. Elaine Maduli was the ringleader of an immigrant smuggling and prostitution network throughout the Western United States, including California and Nevada. She would use smuggled sex workers in her brothels. These workers would be transported into the U.S. through secret crossings at the border or by means of fraudulently obtained visas. The workers would typically owe fees of thousands of dollars to the "snakehead," the smuggler who arranged their entry. The workers were required to pay the debt by working as prostitutes. The women would usually stay two or three weeks at a brothel and then be relocated to a new house, often in different states. The criminal organization used some of the proceeds from the brothels to cover expenses, which included the recruitment of women and the costs to bring them into the United States. The brothel owner would often transfer money from banks in the U.S. to banks in the Philippines. During the one-year period before Ms. Maduli's arrest, approximately $350,000 was wired to banks in the Philippines.

Each brothel would have a manager under Ms. Maduli's authority. The manager would maintain the records for each house and deposit money into the bank. Ms. Maduli would direct the house managers when to move the workers from house to house. They might drive them to the airport for transport to a different city or to different houses in the same city. Ms. Maduli, known as "Madam Boss," was arrested in the Los Angeles area, but indicted in Nevada. My colleague, Ben

Jacobson, and I were hired to represent her. We visited her in federal jail in Nevada. This frail, older woman was handcuffed during our visit. At one point, she easily slipped her right hand out of the cuff, reached into her bra and pulled out a letter to give to her husband. She then put her tiny hand back into the handcuff.

We appeared at the post-indictment arraignment. Ms. Maduli's bond was set at $250,000, well above her means. The indictment alleged she and others transported illegal workers into the U.S. from Laos, Thailand and Indonesia. She was accused of transporting the women through interstate commerce to engage in prostitution. In addition to round-the-clock surveillance, federal officers wiretapped her phones. Operation Exotic Jade was a protracted investigation carried out by the FBI, the Immigration and Naturalization Service and local police. The wiretaps captured Ms. Maduli's illegal activity with incriminating conversations spoken in Tagalog. A transcript in English was provided by the United States Attorney's Office. Dozens of my client's telephone calls with managers of brothels were recorded on the wiretaps. There were some conversations she had with snakeheads, detailing the requirements of her brothels. For example, if she needed two workers in a Northern California brothel, she would have the smuggler bring the workers to Northern California. If some of the girls were unhappy or difficult, she would move them. If workers were sick or unable to perform, she would have them rest or taken to the doctor. Her duties included ensuring the workers satisfied the customers' needs. She ran the operation in the manner of a CEO of a Fortune 500 company. It was clear from the wiretaps she was the owner of these brothels.

We told the court that Ms. Maduli was orphaned at age twelve and moved alone to Manila to work in a sweatshop. She came from a part of the world more tolerant of prostitution. Based on all the separate acts and the brothels she owned, ultimately, if convicted, her prison exposure was in excess of twenty years. This, coupled with the fact that she had a similar case pending against her in federal court in Sacramento, resulted in enough pressure on the client to accept a plea bargain of forty-eight months in prison to be served concurrently for both cases, minus the year she had already spent in custody.

* * * * * * * *

"I'm not Superman," I told the middle-aged Chinese woman sitting across from me. She wanted a guarantee that I would get her case dismissed. She was charged with agreeing to an act of prostitution, a second offense. She advertised sexual services on Craigslist, answered the undercover officer's phone call, set up the appointment, met the officer at an apartment, accepted $160, took off her clothes, placed a condom on the officer and began massaging his genitals. And she wanted a guarantee that I would get the case dismissed!

A similar scene plays out in my office about five times per week. The crime might be different; maybe it is a petty theft, spousal abuse or a drug case, but the question is always the same, "Can you guarantee a dismissal?" Since criminal lawyers are not ethically permitted to guarantee a result, the potential client should hear "no guarantee" in every law office in America. If every lawyer were principled, the client requiring a guarantee would never be able to hire a lawyer. An ethical, decent lawyer convinces the client that a guarantee is impossible. How could any human guarantee a future event? Unscrupulous attorneys promise the world to the client. When they cannot deliver, they insist it is the client's fault. "Well, you weren't truthful with me," they tell the client. Clients are sometimes untruthful with the lawyer and attorneys know it from the outset. Many clients feel they have to withhold their culpability from the lawyer to ensure the lawyer works hard. The client thinks, "If the lawyer knows I am really guilty, he won't give his best effort." Lawyers who practice in the immigrant communities are very familiar with this, and unfortunately some have taken to promising 99% they will get the case dismissed. This is unethical.

A second conviction of prostitution is punishable in California by a mandatory minimum of forty-five days in the county jail, a third offense by a minimum of ninety days. I told a different client there was no way a prosecutor would outright dismiss a second prostitution charge. Her only chance was by going to trial, and that was risky because the judge could sentence her to a lengthy jail term if she lost. There is "no guarantee." She understood the only dismissal scenario was through a trial and even that was a long shot. She did not want to go to jail, but believed another conviction would hinder her chances of getting a green card. The case was prosecuted in a county east of Los Angeles. The arresting officer was a tall handsome black man, whom the client liked. I wondered if part of her desire to have a trial was to see her accuser again.

I fought the case pretrial as long as I could, getting nowhere in negotiations with the prosecutor's office. The case was getting old and we were ordered to trial. The client paid me and I declared ready. We were sent to the master calendar court. I have known this judge for years and he usually leans heavily on the defendant to take a deal. I prepared my client to be aware that the judge might be rude and try to frighten her, but not to worry. The judge puts on an act to force settlements. Surprisingly, the judge said nothing to the client, just transferring the case for trial to Department S. The trial judge resembled an old hippie, complete with long hair flowing down his back. He took the prosecutor and me into chambers to discuss trial issues. Looking at the prosecutor, he said, "Frankly I do not like these cases. As I get older, I've become less comfortable with punishment for this activity." I was astounded. The judge gave the prosecutor a chance to challenge him and be reassigned to another courtroom. To his credit, the prosecutor said he believed the judge would be fair to both sides. The judge told us a story. When he headed the Criminal Division of a local City Attorney's Office, vice officers answered prostitution advertisements by calling the listed phone numbers. The officers concentrated on numbers outside the jurisdiction of their city. The detectives would invite the sex workers to a local hotel. They would then obtain the prostitution violation in their city and submit the case to the City Attorney's Office for filing. The judge said, "I refused to file those cases. I admonished the vice officers that our job is to keep crime out of this city, not bring it in. Don't ever give me these cases again."

My client was charged with two counts, soliciting or agreeing to an act of prostitution, California Penal Code Section 647(b), and loitering for purposes of prostitution, California Penal Code Section 653.22. Loitering for purposes of prostitution requires the defendant have no lawful business at the place where she is thought to be loitering. In this case, my client was an employee of a massage parlor, where she turned on lights, cleaned floors, watered plants, washed towels, lit incense and answered the phone. She clearly had lawful reasons to be present at the location. In chambers, we discussed this issue. The judge agreed with my reasoning and asked the prosecutor why he insisted on proceeding with this charge. He told the prosecutor that if the evidence was consistent with Perliss' offer of proof, he would likely dismiss the loitering count.

Any time after the prosecution rests its case, the defense can make a motion to dismiss based on an insufficiency of the evidence, pursuant to California Penal Code Section 1118.1. The prosecutor sought to keep the loitering charge because, under California law, he was permitted to show the defendant's prior conviction for prostitution as evidence that she was loitering for such purposes. Under the prostitution charge, he was not permitted to bring in the prior, as it would be considered too prejudicial.

I told the judge in chambers that counsel's plan was an obvious attempt to prejudice the jury by getting the prior prostitution conviction into evidence using the loitering count which he knew would be dismissed. The judge agreed and looking at the prosecutor said, "If the loitering count gets dismissed 1118.1, the prejudicial impact of the prior conviction on the prostitution count will be impossible to ignore. Are you willing to live with the consequences?" The prosecutor understood and said, "Yes, I'm willing to take that risk." Before we started with evidence, I approached the undercover officer and told him, "My client likes you, thinks you're handsome." Maybe, I thought, he would go easy on her from the witness stand.

As I cross-examined the officer, I asked many questions about my client's activities. He observed her fold towels, move the massage tables in place and answer the phone several times. I was demonstrating my client's lawful presence at the location. The officer had no idea why I asked these questions. Had he known, I am certain he would not have been so helpful. When the prosecutor rested his case, I moved 1118.1 to dismiss Count Two, the loitering charge. I argued to the court that the activities my client performed proved she had a lawful purpose to be at the location. The judge agreed and dismissed Count

Two. Then I made a motion to dismiss the case entirely because since Count Two was gone, the prejudicial impact of the evidence of her prior now before the jury was incurable. "You cannot put toothpaste back in the tube, you cannot unring the bell," I argued. "Perliss is right," the judge told the prosecutor, who retorted, "You can give a limiting instruction telling the jury not to consider it." The judge laughed, "The defendant is charged with the same crime with which she was previously convicted. How could they not consider it? Impossible." He declared a mistrial and dismissed the case.

* * * * * * * *

Traditional acupuncture, acupressure and massage therapy are interwoven in the Chinese community. With all this touching, sometimes sexual activity results. Prostitution is the solicitation and/or the performing of a sex act for money. I handle two types of prostitution cases. First, there is the direct, obvious case where one advertises sex on the Internet, using language such as "Sexy Asian Woman Wants to Massage all over Your Body." A customer, known as a "John," would call the number advertised, arrive at an apartment, condo, house or hotel room and engage in whatever type of sex he wanted, so long as he was willing to pay the right fee. Often an undercover officer would reply to an Internet ad, and then arrest the sex worker after they met and a discussion of sex for money had occurred. The other type of prostitution case I see is more subtle. It occurs in massage parlors. Typically a customer enters and pays $50 for a legitimate massage. Toward the end of the massage, there would be a discussion about a "happy ending," a sexual favor from the masseuse in exchange for an added tip of perhaps another $50. Very often this extra service is just the touching of the customer's genitals, but sometimes it is more. This occurs inside a business where there are other rooms and customers.

The Vice Squad, now often called the Morals Unit, will send an undercover officer into a massage parlor as a John. During the massage, the officer will make small talk with the masseuse. The massage starts on the undercover officer's back. The masseuse might ask if the customer feels good or the officer might volunteer how relaxed he is. Maybe the officer would tell the masseuse how pretty she is or how special her touch is. The masseuse might say the officer is handsome or strong. Either the masseuse hints at an extra service or the officer just says it, "How about a little extra? How much would that cost?" The officer will make sure money is mentioned. Most massage therapists would reject this request. A few might start to touch the officer intimately, or prepare to do so by putting extra oil on her hands or by pulling off the towel. Sometimes the officer allows the masseuse to touch him sexually for a little while, then stops it with a pretext, a need for a trip to the bathroom or water or a coughing fit. When the officer has enough evidence, he will signal awaiting backup officers. The officer might have a wire hidden in his shirt, hanging on a hook a few feet away.

I tried a prostitution case for a licensed masseuse in Los Angeles County Superior Court. At the beginning of the trial, I questioned the jurors about whether they had any prejudices that would influence their ability to be fair. One of the jurors was a radiologist, a bearded man wearing a suit. I left him on the jury hoping, as a doctor, he would be more understanding of the human condition than others. The undercover officer was the first witness. He testified he had been involved in at least thirty similar cases. He made the mistake of saying, "They're all the same." He told his story. He was a big man, 6'3, 300 lbs. I have had other cases with him, become friendly with him, and most importantly, I learned he is a little too cocky on the witness stand. Once I jokingly asked him if his wife received her subpoena. I told him I had subpoenaed her to court during his testimony. He said something about my needing to drive carefully lest I get pulled over for a minor traffic violation.

Cross-examination of the officer revealed he did not record his conversation with the masseuse. Before he went to the location, he met with four other officers, including two detectives at the police department to lay out his undercover strategy. They planned the operation and each officer's role. He testified there were roughly twenty-five officers on duty at any given time and that five officers and four police cars were used in this investigation. He conceded that when he entered the location, his intent was to engage the masseuse in a conversation about sex, then obtain the prostitution violation. The officer testified he usually used a wire to alert backup officers, but on this occasion did not. According to him, the one wire owned by the police department was in use for another investigation. He acknowledged the words spoken during the negotiation were evidence of criminal conduct and that using a recorder could have captured those words. He said, however, it was too inconvenient to use a recorder. I asked him, "Wouldn't it be better for the jury to hear the actual words, so they could make this important decision themselves rather than just rely on your testimony?" He disagreed. I said, "You want the jury to hear the conversation exclusively through you, while you intentionally allowed the actual evidence to dissipate into thin air." He disagreed again, saying he could not record due to officer safety, as if this 6'3" 300 pound officer were somehow afraid of the tiny Asian female sitting next to me. I asked in the most leading and argumentative way, "If you wanted the jury to know the truth, you would have recorded the incident and played it for them." At this point the judge sustained the DA's objection. No matter, the jury already knew the answer.

The DA put into evidence the newspaper containing the defendant's advertisement. It was one of those free weekly papers where erotic services are advertised. The ad for my client's massage parlor was very small, "Professional Massage Services," displaying the address, phone number and the $50 per hour fee. The other ads were suggestive such as "Hot Sexy Asian Masseuse Will Give You the Massage of Your Dreams" or "Sexy Beautiful Chinese Woman." Handing the newspaper to the officer, the DA asked him to show my client's advertisement to the jury. The DA had not realized that my client's ad was the least provocative. It was the only one which did not flagrantly suggest sex. I spent an afternoon cross-examining the officer about every nasty ad. I started in the left hand corner of the paper and pointed to the ad saying "Hot Sexy Asian." I asked, "Was *this one* my client's?" Of course, we already knew it was not. I asked the same question for each explicit ad and in each question, I would recite the sexually stimulating wording: "Hot Sexy Asian Will Make you Come Home in Ecstasy"; "Curvaceous Babe will Release all your Tensions"; "Full Body Satisfaction." I was coaxing the jury into contrasting my client's modest ad with the more explicit ads I was reading aloud. For each of these ads, the officer had to admit the ad was not my client's. I was having a good time projecting my voice and catching the full attention of the jury, when I noticed the judge from the adjoining courtroom standing in the back hallway poking his head around the door behind the witness stand. Here was Judge Wayne Miller laughing at my carrying on. He had recognized my voice. Since our first meeting in Baumann's office, he and I became good friends after our wives met at a local school event. Seeing him laughing at my ridiculous cross-examination caused me to laugh as well. Regaining my composure, I asked the officer to read to the jury the ad in which he found my client. He read it: "Professional Massage Services."

"Doesn't it seem unusual that the most modest ad would be picked for a sting operation?"

"No."

"My client's ad does not suggest sexual services."

"Well, she would not be advertising in this newspaper if it were a professional massage."

"Isn't there something else notable about my client's simple advertisement compared with the obviously sexually-toned ads that dominate the paper?"

"No."

"Isn't it true that in my client's ad, her address appears, while in all the other ads just a phone number is listed?"

"Yeah, so what?"

The jury could see firsthand the brash officer losing his composure. I called my client to the witness stand. She had been a licensed masseuse for five years. She paid for the requisite classes and successfully completed the massage therapist school. She passed the therapist exam and received her license. Adamantly denying the officer's accusations, she testified in Chinese, through an interpreter, crying the entire duration of her testimony. She was crying so hard she had fluids coming from every orifice of her face. She was putting on quite a show.

The evidence phase of the trial ended and I presented my final argument. I reminded the jury that it was the prosecutor's burden to prove guilt beyond a reasonable doubt, and that the evidence must leave each juror with an abiding conviction of guilt before a guilty verdict could be rendered. I pointed out that "abiding" means long lasting, and that "conviction" is defined as a religious-like belief. You cannot find someone guilty and then later think maybe you made a mistake. You have to truly believe in your heart the DA proved the case beyond a reasonable doubt. I went on and on about this principle and then summarized the facts of the case. I highlighted the disproportionate use of the police department's resources, using one-fifth of the available on-duty officers in such a silly investigation. Then I took a small $25 recording device from my pocket. I held it up before the jury and said that, with all the resources the police used to arrest this young woman, they apparently did not have the funds to buy a $25 tape recorder. "So you, Ladies and Gentlemen of the jury, charged with the duty of deciding whether the prosecution has shown sufficient evidence to convict beyond a reasonable doubt, are deprived of listening to what actually happened. Instead, you are asked to rubber stamp what the officer claims happened. Thank God we live in America, where jurors decide facts, not police officers. Incidentally, why do you suppose the officer testified, 'They're all the same'?"

I saved my best argument for last. The officer had flippantly testified that someone else was using the wire, so he could not. Looking out the corner of my eye at the radiologist, I continued, "Can you imagine, you go to the doctor complaining of terrible back pain? The doctor says he's seen this thirty times before and each time it's the same, *you* definitely need back surgery. What? I need back surgery? Shouldn't we take x-rays or something just to be sure?" The doctor says, 'Nah, someone else is using the x-ray machine anyway.'" I glanced at the radiologist. He was laughing. He knew I was talking to *him*. The jury came back with a not guilty verdict.

* * * * * * * *

I was in the courthouse appearing on a drunk-driving case when I ran into Attorney Max Tu, a friend and outstanding civil lawyer, who sometimes defends a criminal case. He is fearless, ready to handle any type of case, but respects my background and experience, and sometimes refers criminal matters to me. Max was in court on a prostitution case set for trial. He noticed me walk in the courtroom and asked if I would look at his file. He was about to start trial and wanted my advice. I reviewed the file and told him it was a difficult case, that his only chance was to cross-examine the undercover officer as to the language barrier and the failure to record the conversation, thus allowing the evidence to dissipate. Max asked if I would do the trial. I told Max I was certain he would do a great job and I was unprepared. I had just read the file and the jury panel was waiting outside the courtroom. With a busy civil caseload, Max was visibly anxious about spending so much time in trial. I did not have a heavy calendar for the next several days and I was itching to do something challenging. It would only be a two-day trial. I took the case. Knowing my reputation as a criminal defense attorney, the client agreed to the substitution.

The client was a pleasant looking Chinese lady. I attempted to fill the jury with as many men as possible. Women jurors are tougher than men on female sex workers. The client was a masseuse, accused of offering a "happy ending" to an undercover officer. There was not a lot to the case. I knew both the DA and the judge well. While amused I took the case on short notice, they both respected me and were confident the case would go smoothly. The officer testified that he wore a wire, but neglected to record the words proving the defendant's offer of a happy ending. Once he heard the offer, he testified, "I spoke the code words over the wire to alert the backup officers that the violation had occurred and to enter and arrest the defendant."

The code words were, "Who's your Daddy?" The officer told the masseuse to say these words when giving him a sexual favor. The backup officers would hear this and enter the premises. It must have been too complicated for the backup officers to hear the entire conversation, and at the same time, turn on a recording device to preserve the evidence. The bailiff, a very funny man, asked me to teach him how to say "Who's your Daddy?" in Chinese. From then on, he would tease my client by saying it to her in Mandarin. Sometimes, a lawyer tries to bring levity to a courtroom drama, making the defendant more human. In this case, the bailiff did it for me.

I cross-examined the officer about the quantity of resources used for the investigation and that the police department, as in my previous case, apparently could not afford a $25 recording device. I examined him about the client's problem understanding English. Finally, I asked what he expected to happen once he set the investigation into motion. I suggested he perceived only what he expected and did not consider any alternative explanations.

In closing, I argued that the defendant's innocent conduct was confused with guilty behavior because the officer was predisposed to believing the defendant was a sex worker. An undercover officer will usually use suggestive language to obtain a sex-for-money agreement. The problem is that the officers typically only speak English and the masseuse speaks Mandarin. Perhaps she is innocently agreeing to incomprehensible words. The masseuse does not understand the customer, but nods in agreement to be pleasant, not necessarily for sex. This is innocent conduct interpreted as guilty behavior. I illustrated for the jury the problem of the officer's expectations and perception with a story.

"There was an enchanting kingdom in Central Europe ruled by a benevolent king. The people prospered and the king was greatly loved. There was one man, however, who hated the king and plotted to overthrow his kingdom. He was the king's wicked brother, who amassed an army and ultimately defeated the king's forces. The benevolent king fled to a neighboring land where he remained quietly in hiding. As time passed, he became friendly with the townsfolk, decent and loving neighbors. One of the people in the town stood out. Today, we would not talk this way, but in those days people might say he was the 'village idiot.' This man would walk around town declaring, 'I am the king.' The townsfolk humored him. One villager made a wooden crown for him. Another sewed common linens into a cloak. Another made a scepter from an old animal bone. On one extremely horrible day, while the townsfolk were gathered at a meeting, they were quickly surrounded by menacing soldiers with swords drawn. 'We are looking for the king.' When the village idiot heard this, he immediately stood and declared, 'I am the king.' The soldiers encircled the man, bound him and prepared to execute him. The benevolent king could not stand to see another die in his place, so he rose, stepped in front of the soldiers and in his most authoritarian voice announced, 'The man you seek is me, for I am the true king.' The soldiers, upon hearing and seeing this, immediately pushed him aside saying, 'You are just trying to protect your king.' They proceeded to kill the village idiot. If the soldiers had looked more carefully, they would have seen the crown was amateurishly made of poor quality wood; the cloak was common linen and the scepter an old animal bone. Had they been paying attention, they would have realized the village idiot's voice and enunciation was childish. They simply did not notice. They were there to see the king, and it was the king they saw, no matter the proof to the contrary. The soldiers found what they were predisposed to see, just as the undercover officer in this case heard what he was predisposed to hear."

The judge instructed the jury and they retired to the jury room for deliberations. After a full morning of deliberation, they signaled the judge they were hopelessly deadlocked. The judge declared a mistrial and dismissed the case, refusing to retry it.

* * * * * * * *

The three preceding cases all involved massage professionals accused of a sex act of merely touching or agreeing to touch the private parts of an undercover officer during a massage. California Penal Code Section 647(b) treats all types of prostitution the same, whether it be simple touching while inside the confines of a private massage room or completed intercourse in a publicly accessible bathroom. I believe a person who commits such victimless crimes in a private setting should not be subjected to criminal penalties. Often unskilled immigrants have difficulty finding employment. How can they be blamed for wanting a better life? They need to survive, feed, clothe, shelter and educate their children. Whom are they hurting? Yet society demonizes them simply for using survival skills. Why is free sexual activity between consenting adults legal, while the same conduct for money illegal? I mentioned my opinion of prostitution to a female DA who told me that prostitution by its very nature is not victimless, but in fact a crime against women. I thought, the police send a male undercover officer to encourage a masseuse to touch him inappropriately for money, and then arrests her. She comes to court and the DA wants her to suffer a conviction and additional jail time. Damn right this woman's a victim. She's a victim of the DA, the cops and the criminal justice system.

It is very easy to hate those who are unpopular. The word "criminal" has become a catalyst for hatred. We apply the word to those we consider horrible, evil people. In the late 1940s and throughout the 1950s, during the McCarthy years, Americans hated the communists. Now we sometimes target our hatred toward petty criminals. Too many of our tax dollars are used to incarcerate people. The State of California spends $40,000 a year per inmate and $10,000 annually for each K-12 student. Of course, there are people who must be imprisoned, but I question the need to incarcerate sex workers, or those who have problems with drugs or mental disorders. There used to be ample mental hospitals and clinics. Few such mental health centers exist today, especially in California. We pigeonhole many people under the label of criminal. We shun and abhor them. We despise illegal "aliens"; we've become a society that thrives on being judgmental. Our least fortunate are not our enemies. In the profound space between our minds and our hearts, we can create a more inclusive society.

The attorney knows his or her client as a person. As the attorney, you alone stand between your client and prison, or in some cases, the death penalty. Society has little sympathy for the individual, indulging instead in judgmentalism and the collective catharsis of revenge and punishment. The attorney bears the burden and sole responsibility of helping those labeled "criminals," such as those whose only crime may be the exchanging of money for sex. To force anyone to engage in sex is reprehensible and criminal. However, in a free society, it should be a purely private matter when consenting adults participate in a sex-for-money transaction. The attorney goes to court and faces a tough, occasionally uncompromising DA and the rare judge who might simply rubber-stamp the prosecutor, completely ignoring his or her "detached and neutral" role. At times the attorney feels everyone is a prosecutor. In daily discourse, in coffee houses, restaurants, nightclubs, bowling alleys and shopping malls, one too often hears hatred spewing against society's "enemies." Defending the least powerful can be a lonely enterprise.

* * * * * * * *

I represented a client accused of aiding and abetting a brothel owner, commonly called a pimp. My client drove customers to and from the brothel. He was a simple man, although aware of the criminal nature of the enterprise. When business was slow, the sex workers would badger him to get them clients. More customers meant more money to the sex worker. The pimp earns hundreds of thousands of dollars per year, the sex workers $50 per client. The police were monitoring and surveilling various members of the operation. With search warrants in hand, police entered the brothel while the pimp was away. Three low level employees were arrested: my client, a cleaning person and a tea server. All were minimum wage employees and all had aided and abetted the crime of pimping. The sex workers were not charged. They were considered material witnesses for testimony against those arrested. My client was at the bottom of the totem pole, but he was charged with aiding and abetting the crime of pimping, under California Penal Code Section 266h. He was prosecuted with the same vigor with which a pimp would be prosecuted. Since the crime of pimping requires a mandatory prison term, the DA's office sought a state prison sentence for this minimum wage earner, while the prostitutes feigned victimhood and the pimp escaped justice altogether. Under California law, all three defendants aided and abetted the crime and were equally guilty of pimping. Avoiding state prison was impossible. However, the DA agreed to a lesser pimping crime under California Penal Code Section 266f, reducing the defendants' punishment from the mandatory minimum of three years to an agreed upon disposition of two years state prison, one year of actual time to be served.

* * * * * * * *

When one aids and abets a crime and has knowledge of the criminal intent and enterprise of the principal, he is equally guilty of the criminal conduct. But what if one unknowingly aids and abets a crime, and thereafter acts in a way perceived as consistent with a consciousness of guilt? This happened in the case of Alvin Salcido.

It was a laid back Saturday night. Alvin drove his friends around the neighborhood looking for some action, perhaps a few girls to party with. As the car approached a group of partiers outside an apartment complex, Alvin's passenger pulled a handgun from inside his jacket and shot into the crowd killing a man. "What the *hell* did you do that for?" Alvin screamed at his passenger, as he accelerated, fleeing the scene. Later he lied to detectives, saying he was not there. Along with the shooter, Alvin was charged with murder, punishable by life in prison. I was appointed to represent him. I met with the backseat passengers and listened to their stories. I brought them to the DA and detective. They related that no one but the shooter knew of the gun and what Alvin had said immediately after the shot was fired. The detective thought they were just trying to shield Alvin. However, recognizing the weakness in the case, the DA agreed Alvin could plead guilty to the crime of accessory after the fact, California Penal Code Section 32. Alvin received a jolt of jail time as a condition of his felony probation.

Why wasn't Alvin guilty of murder as an aider and abettor? Alvin and the two back seat passengers knew nothing of the gun. They did not knowingly assist in the shooting. However, after the shooting, they fled the scene, behavior implying a guilty mind. What saved Alvin was his statement immediately after the shot was fired. "What the hell did you do that for?" demonstrated Alvin's ignorance of the shooter's plan to fire into a crowd. Alvin was guilty of fleeing the scene and removing the shooter from the location. This is a classic example of an "accessory after the fact," a crime punishable by no more than three years in state prison, in contrast to life in prison for aiding and abetting a murder.

Chapter VI

Breaking and Entering the Global Cookie Jar: Theft & Fraud

Young criminal lawyers aspire to try by jury as many cases as possible. For lawyers, experience is gold. A lawyer's courtroom instinct, mental reflexes and creativity are fine-tuned by participating in jury trials. The attorney learns to analyze facts to weave into defense strategies and theories, to best present proof, cross-examine witnesses and confidently attack the opponent's case. Some untested lawyers may take a small fee to resolve a case prematurely, even though knowledge and wisdom dictate perseverance for the most favorable result. They fear what is unfamiliar: a jury trial.

An adept trial lawyer's mind is working to perceive the slight nuances in the evidence. She is aggressive with the presentation of the smallest of details, which can sway the jury to her side. In a recent prostitution case, a defendant hired me after she became dissatisfied with a young lawyer. The lawyer wanted her to plead guilty to the charge. After reading through the discovery, I agreed there was ample evidence she had offered and initiated a sex act with the undercover officer. But there was no evidence of a discussion about, or an exchange of money, a necessary element for the crime of prostitution. The earlier lawyer did not recognize the absence of this essential aspect of the crime. I declared ready for trial, knowing I would win. The prosecutor dismissed the case.

Representing clients charged with a wide spectrum of crimes enhances an attorney's skills. One comes to understand what on the surface may seem like a losing case, might not necessarily be hopeless at all. A sharp criminal defense attorney will try to put herself in the shoes of the prosecutor, and then ask herself, as *DA*, "what are my weaknesses in this case?" Rather than just attempt to fit the facts into an already thought out defense, he or she looks for holes in a prosecutor's case, then exposes and amplifies those defects. To forcefully attack the prosecutor's case is the best strategy to succeed at trial. The law gives the prosecutor a high burden of proof, beyond a reasonable doubt. The more the prosecutor's case is challenged, the better. The prosecutor's case is like a chain, made of disparate links, each attached to the next. Weakening the links causes the chain to fall apart. The following trial is an example of weak links leading to a dismissal.

I represented Maggie Tang, charged along with her cousin with immigration fraud. Her cousin was running an immigration-consulting business. He would use false documents to assist his clients in applying for legal status. He violated California law when he used counterfeit official seals as originals. He was charged in Superior Court with multiple felony forgeries and fraud.

Maggie did the accounting for the business. She went to trial with her cousin and a third defendant, all accused of defrauding a client of $40,000. The cousin had promised to return a $50,000 fee, should they fail to obtain a social security card for the client. Only $10,000 was refunded. Most of the evidence implicated the two other defendants and not Maggie. While working in the office, she had taken some sealed envelopes from clients to be delivered to her cousin. There was no evidence she knew the contents. She was not involved with the preparation of any of the immigration petitions. When law enforcement investigated the crimes, they arrested the three employees at the business, thinking all were involved.

In trial, it became evident Maggie was simply the bookkeeper for the business. My examination of the witnesses made it clear that Maggie was not present when any of the fee retainers were read or signed. She was not involved in the preparation of the fraudulent activity. The trial for Maggie ended with the judge granting an 1118.1 motion. This motion is appropriate when the evidence does not rise to the level required to support a conviction beyond a reasonable doubt. The judge exercised his power and took the case from the jury, acquitting Maggie.

My co-counsel was Ben Jacobson, a prominent defense lawyer who represented Maggie's cousin. Ben has been a friend since the mid-80s, when we both served on the Board of the Los Angeles Criminal Courts Bar Association, the largest local association of criminal lawyers in California. Both born and raised in the Detroit area, we have many friends and interests in common.

Ben was a member of the Beverly Hills Tennis Club. He took me as a guest and suggested I join. It is important for people in high stress jobs to have an outlet, both physical and emotional. To me, tennis is an exhilarating exercise, whereas working out in a gym is boring. I visited the club with Ben and met the sales representative, Mary. A major selling point was that the club's tennis pro evaluated each member, grouping him or her with other players of equal skill. When a member wanted a game, he or she would call the club and arrange a match. With my unusual schedule of being in court early in the morning and in my law offices in the later afternoon, the late mornings and early afternoons were often open for play. I listened incredulously as Mary claimed that a benefit of joining was seeing famous tennis players in action. She told me professional players, such as Jimmy Connors, had recently played there. She could tell I didn't believe her. I joined anyway and started playing five times a week. Three months later, while walking toward the clubhouse past the tennis courts, I observed a crowd milling around center court. Mary was there and saw me coming. With a big smile on her face, she motioned me over. Pointing to center court, she said, "Look." Playing there was my tennis hero, Bjorn Borg. In the middle of the match, Mary took my hand and walked me down the steps and onto the court. She escorted me up to Borg and introduced us, "Mr. Borg, I want you to meet Sandy Perliss, one of our new members." Borg extended his right hand, and in his thick Swedish accent replied, "Nice to meet you." I was in shock. I went to the locker room, changed, played a couple hours of tennis and came back to the locker room. Borg's locker was next to mine. Not only had I met him, but to my surprise, here standing next to me was Bjorn Borg in his birthday suit.

* * * * * * * *

My client in the following immigration fraud case was not as fortunate as Maggie Tang. Saniel Han purchased another's identity from an American living in China. After six years of living in Los Angeles, he missed his family. He did not dare return to China for fear his true identity would be discovered upon re-entry to the United States. He had a California driver's license with his new name, social security card and birth certificate. He needed a passport. Having what he believed was sufficient proof, he applied to the U.S. Passport Office. His brother warned against this, saying it was too risky. Saniel would not listen. His brother's suspicions worsened when Saniel received a call from the passport office advising that his passport was ready for pickup from the Federal Building. His brother did not believe the authorities called each passport applicant. Saniel still would not listen, went to the passport office and was promptly arrested and charged in the United States District Court with submitting false documents. His brother hired me. There was not a lot I could do. Saniel had confessed the whole story to investigators. We worked out a plea agreement for six months in custody, after which, of course, Saniel would be deported. Now he misses Los Angeles, but at least he is with his family.

After I defended Saniel, I represented a foreign national investigated in a twenty-five million dollar Medi-Cal fraud case. Javier Ballesteros was a businessman from Portugal. He hired a local bookkeeper to run his company in the City of Industry. The bookkeeper spoke perfect Portuguese and broken English, and was unfamiliar with many of the tax withholding and worker compensation laws. When the state taxing authority learned the company was not complying with tax regulations, Javier was criminally charged with three years of non-withholding of taxes. There were twelve felony tax violation charges, one for each quarter. When Javier returned to the United States, he was arrested on the twelve felony counts. He was not acquainted with any criminal defense lawyers, but knew a civil lawyer whose office was down the street from Javier's warehouse. The civil lawyer appeared at the arraignment and advised Javier to plead guilty to all twelve charges, with each count carrying a maximum of three years' prison. The case was set for sentencing a month later.

When Javier came to me, he had already pleaded guilty. I studied the complaint, astounded that an attorney would plead Javier guilty on all twelve counts. Usually, when someone accepts a plea bargain, he pleads guilty to one or two charges and the remaining counts are dismissed. This was a man who had no criminal record and an ongoing business. He had delegated the bookkeeping responsibilities to someone he trusted.

I advised Javier to pay the past due taxes immediately, so we could go to the judge with ammunition of good will. I went to see the sentencing judge in Department 100 of the Criminal Courts Building. I had known this judge for some years. During a break, the DA and I approached the Bench. I told the judge Javier's story, that he had used a civil lawyer who pleaded him guilty to all these counts and the sentencing was coming to this court in a week. I told the judge I wanted to withdraw the plea. I argued that he was a foreigner, unaware of the bookkeeper's malfeasance. The judge told me to hold off withdrawing the plea, saying he would drop eleven of the felony charges and change the remaining charge to a misdemeanor at the time of sentencing. My client would just pay a fine. I said that would do it. I advised my client of the conversation. Several weeks later, we went to court for sentencing. The judge, true to his word, dismissed eleven of the felony counts and made the twelfth a misdemeanor, ordering my client to pay a fine. That was the end of it. Javier was appreciative. He took me to his offices and showed me around, telling me he wanted me to be the company's lawyer. I toured his warehouse. He had many boxes filled with unfamiliar products. I learned that he was selling adult diapers and incontinence supplies.

When the story broke of the largest Medi-Cal fraud in California history, I immediately realized what Javier was doing. The fraud involved using elderly Medi-Cal recipients' identification numbers to bill the state for the sale of huge quantities of incontinence supplies. Administrators running retirement homes, assisted-living homes and elderly care outpatient clinics helped to provide the Medi-Cal identification numbers to vendors. Some supplies were provided, but the state was billed thousands of dollars more for undelivered products. On the day the authorities arrested twelve Medi-Cal fraud suspects, Javier was at home in Portugal. After Javier heard about the bust from his bookkeeper, he never returned to the United States. I defended a half dozen of these cases throughout the state. I went to Sacramento, San Bernardino, San Diego and Orange County. These cases all involved suspects friendly with Javier. Upon arrest, they received word from Javier's bookkeeper that I was the right lawyer to contact. So between the years of 1990 and 1993, I was traveling the state representing Medi-Cal defendants.

* * * * * * * *

Taylor Wei was one of those Medi-Cal defendants; he called me after speaking to Javier's bookkeeper. He owned a large Medi-Cal supply company, which sold incontinence supplies throughout the State of California. Taylor used the same procedures that had gotten so many others in trouble. He was on bail when he came to my office. His massive case with dozens of allegations was pending in Superior Court in Northern California. The total loss to the State of California was over six million dollars; Taylor's substantial bank accounts were accordingly frozen by the State Attorney General's Office. Having had similar cases, I knew how to unfreeze the accounts, so long as no court seizure order was served on the bank. I took the necessary steps to unfreeze the accounts. But within minutes, Los Angeles County Sheriff Deputies served a seizure warrant on the bank account, signed by a Los Angeles Superior Court judge.

I went to court in Northern California to represent the client. The scheme was the same as Javier's. Taylor was billing Medi-Cal for supplies he was not delivering. He was getting access to patients' identification numbers through convalescent homes and the like. The prosecuting authority was the State of California Attorney General's Office. The case lasted six months and resulted in an agreement whereby much of the money was repaid from Taylor's seized bank accounts, the client receiving ninety days of house arrest. It was a great deal.

While Taylor's case was pending, I handled another smaller Medi-Cal fraud case where I was able to reach a similar agreement. Many such cases were going on. At one point, the number two man in the Attorney General's Office Medi-Cal Fraud Unit approached me at the Los Angeles Criminal Courts Building downtown and angrily told me that I would not be getting such lenient deals any more. Two months later, I resolved a similar case for one hundred twenty days of house arrest, despite the Attorney General Office's protest. Unfortunately for my next client, a San Bernardino woman charged with Medi-Cal fraud, the outcome was not so fortunate. The Attorney General's Office position met with favor in front of a strict judge who sentenced her to sixteen months in state prison.

These cases occurred in the early 90s. Many in this group of Medi-Cal fraud cases came from the Filipino community of Southern California. I have found these types of schemes tend to plague many ethnic communities. One person invents a new version of this fraud and friends or family members follow suit, like the spread of a virus through a population. Five years later, there was a similar viral spread of this crime throughout the Armenian community in Los Angeles. I began to represent Armenians, but this time it was a little different. The US Attorney was prosecuting them for fraud in Federal Court. I represented one client in the U.S. District Court in Sacramento. We worked out a similar resolution in this case that I was getting in the early 90s. The U.S. Attorney was, at that time, willing to go easy on defendants who repaid the money stolen from the government. Those days are long gone.

* * * * * * * *

Not all theft crimes are major frauds. Robert Williams entered a Target Department Store, selected $800 worth of clothing and brought it to the cashier. He knew the familiar face behind the cash register, having been friends for many years. The cashier rang up the bill and Williams handed him a Target credit card. The entire transaction was watched on closed-circuit television by loss prevention officers, who recognized its fraudulent nature. Security officers arrested Williams after he exited with the clothing. He was charged with grand theft, as was the cashier.

Mr. Williams hired me. Because of his criminal record, a conviction would violate his felony probation and land him in state prison. At the arraignment, I pleaded him not guilty and received the complaint and police reports. I went through the reports with him, asked for and photocopied his Target credit card. The reports described the transaction but were silent as to the actual relationship between Williams and the cashier. After arrest, both Williams and the cashier invoked their Miranda Rights, choosing not to talk. Williams' case was pending before a stern judge. Because Williams was on felony probation, we had no choice but go to trial. Even if Williams pleaded guilty to a lesser charge, his probation officer would recommend that he be found in violation and sent back to prison.

At trial, the loss prevention officer testified his attention was drawn to Williams because he looked suspicious selecting the clothing. I suggested it more likely because he was African American. The loss prevention officer watched on closed circuit TV as Williams approached the cashier, presented his credit card, accepted the receipt and bag of clothes and exited the store. I cross-examined the witness about the credit card.

"That credit card was valid, wasn't it?"

"I have no information to the contrary."

"There is nothing on the face of the credit card showing it to be fraudulent?"

"Correct."

"There have been no suspicious returns on that credit card?"

"None that I am aware of."

"Isn't it true there has been no history of questionable activity on this credit card?"

"That's true."

"You have absolutely no evidence that my client knew or had ever even met that cashier before, correct?"

"I have no such evidence," he said in exasperation. Williams had been arrested while walking out of the store.

"My client did not resist when you detained him, did he?"

"No."

"He didn't make any attempt to flee, did he?"

"No."

I could not let Williams testify because he would be impeached with his prior burglary conviction. Of course, I wanted to keep this from the jury. When I was a DA, my case often improved when defendants took the stand. Most defendants do not hold up well under cross-examination. They make mistakes, are tricked. When a defendant is cross-examined, psychologically, the burden seems to shift to the defense, even though, under the law, it is the prosecutor's obligation to prove the case beyond a reasonable doubt. When the defendant takes the stand, the jury is watching his every move, the body language, if he sweats, the way his eyes move, if he appears uncomfortable. It is especially dangerous to put a defendant on the witness stand when he or she will be impeached with a prior record. When the judge asked if I had any witnesses, I stood and said, "Your Honor, the defense has decided to rely on the weight of the evidence." In closing, I argued the DA did not have proof beyond a reasonable doubt. The problem with the DA's case was the absence of proof to support the relationship between Williams and the cashier.

The judge instructed the jury. The reasonable doubt instruction is always read to the jury in a criminal case. They are told that with reasonable doubt, they must find the defendant not guilty. The defendant is always presumed innocent until the prosecution has proven otherwise. The jury must unanimously agree before the defendant can be convicted. The jury in Williams' case was out three hours. They sent a note to the judge that they were deadlocked. The judge brought them out and inquired. They remained divided, and the judge sent them back for further deliberation. Two hours later, the jury indicated nothing had changed. The judge declared a mistrial and asked the foreman the split and direction the jury was leaning. It was eight to four for not guilty. The judge dismissed the case. Williams' probation officer recommended the court not find him in violation of his probation.

* * * * * * * *

*Having no unusual coincidence is far more unusual
than any coincidence could possibly be.*
— Isaac Asimov

In promoting my San Gabriel Valley law office, I met many merchants and members of the local Chamber of Commerce. One member, Rick Pearson, owned an auto body shop. I would take my damaged car for repairs to Rick and sometimes refer a client or friend to his shop. Rick and I became friends and would occasionally play tennis or meet for lunch. One evening, Rick called; his nephew had been arrested for shoplifting. Rick asked if I would take care of him. Accused of removing clothing from a boutique, he was cited for petty theft with a court date three weeks away. I resolved the case with a no contest plea to trespassing, a lesser non-moral turpitude crime. He was sentenced to twelve months of informal probation, after which I petitioned the conviction be dismissed pursuant to Penal Code, Section 1203.4, which was granted.

In gratitude, Rick invited me to a professional hockey game. Knowing I was from Detroit, he purchased tickets for the Detroit Red Wings vs. Los Angeles Kings game. As we talked during the game, I learned Rick spent much of his youth in the American South. I explained I grew up in the Detroit area and until 1981 never lived outside of Michigan, with the exception of a six month internship in Washington, D.C. in my final year of college. As an intern to a member of the United States House of Representatives, I drafted correspondence, researched issues of importance to the constituents and prepared speeches for the congressman. During that internship, I met and dated a small town Alabama girl named Isabel. She was a page on the floor of the House of Representatives. In those days, the duty of a page was to deliver messages between members of Congress and their staff. After I completed my internship, I graduated from college and then attended law school in Los Angeles. I stayed in contact with Isabel. After law school and before the bar exam, I took a road trip to the East Coast, stopping to visit friends along the way. I spent a couple of days with Isabel in Madeline, a town of less than a thousand people. When I arrived, the whole town was cordially waiting for the "boy from L.A." I was telling Rick this story, that the only city I ever visited in the South was Madeline, Alabama. His jaw dropped: "That's where I went to high school!"

* * * * * * * *

President of the Korean American Council of Investment Strategists, Bainbridge Kim had it all: a loving wife, two beautiful daughters, ages ten and eight, a successful investment counseling firm and a fat bank account. One Sunday in late June, Bainbridge took his girls to a shopping mall to purchase towels, swimsuits and a beach bag. The girls chose a clear bag with a pink dolphin decorated on its front. The dolphin would move in water as the girls carried the bag. The price tags dangled as Dad carried the bag around the store. It was a busy day and Dad had to wait in a long line for the cashier. The girls asked if they could play. He said it would be all right, not thinking they would go far. He stayed in line. After a few minutes, he lost sight of his girls. Nervous, he left the line and began walking up and down the aisles, all the time holding the beach bag. His movements and constant looking around made him suspicious to loss prevention officers, who later described him as "furtively" moving about. When, after some time, he still could not find his girls, he became agitated. He left the department store and entered the mall, hurrying to the pet store thinking he might locate the girls there. They always liked playing with the dogs. He was oblivious to the bag he was holding. Four loss prevention officers confronted him, accusing him of leaving the store with stolen goods. He said he was scared his girls were missing and thought maybe they had gone to play at the pet store. The loss prevention officers believed he was stealing. Nevertheless, cognizant of his extreme agitation, they accompanied him to the pet store, where the girls were playing with a puppy. Mr. Kim was then arrested and I was hired.

Mr. Kim was facing theft charges at the Orange County Superior Court. The City Prosecutor would not agree to any negotiated settlement on the case, saying, "It's a slam dunk." Sometimes when a defendant is well off financially, the prosecutor will be vindictively harsher. The thought is that a wealthy man does not need to steal. The reverse take, from the defense position, is that being rich, there is no motive to steal. Usually these two theories are at work opposing each other in a trial of this nature.

The City Prosecutor assigned for trial was Maurice Kelley. Maurice had been a DA before joining a local City Attorney's office in Orange County. We knew each other from the days when I had been a DA. He was a fun-loving, decent guy, a slender black man, a competent adversary. Mr. Kim was likewise a gentleman and understood it was the job of the City Prosecutor to prosecute him and that it was true he had done something suspicious. But he had not intended to steal, only to find his daughters. He recognized from an outside perspective it looked like stealing.

His girls were defense witnesses in the trial. During a break, I took Maurice aside and talked to him on the bench outside the court. The dimple cheeked eight-year-old skipped up to me and proudly displayed the multicolored book she was reading. It was a book with pop outs, appropriate for her age. "Uncle Sandy, will you read to me while we wait?" I said, "Darling, I have something better than that." I picked her up and placed her on Maurice's lap, handing him the book. "Maurice, this lovely little girl needs you to read to her." The jury was curiously looking on as they were waiting outside the courtroom. Maurice had two choices. He could stand up or he could smile and read. He chose to read, showing the jury he was indeed a decent man. He read to her for ten minutes while we waited to resume trial. I had tricked Maurice, putting him in an awkward position. Later, over a couple beers, Maurice and I joked about it.

During the trial, the girls testified about going to play at the pet store. It is difficult for a prosecutor to cross-examine children when the father is in trouble. One does not wish to appear an ogre, using a child to convict his or her own father. One would fear she would grow up thinking she is the reason Daddy went to jail. So in such cross-examination, a prosecutor must be careful. It is a difficult job to accomplish. Prosecutors tend to go easy on child witnesses, because there is little to gain and lots to lose. Maurice, a skilled prosecutor, knew this. On cross-examination, he left the girls alone.

At the end of the evidence phase of the trial, my client leaned over to me and commented that whatever happened with the jury, he wanted to invite the prosecutor to his home for dinner. He wanted his girls to know that Mr. Kelley was an honorable person doing his job, that his mission was important and had a worthy purpose. He especially did not want the girls to dislike the prosecutor because he was black. The jury found Mr. Kim not guilty. Several of the jurors would comment later that they were bothered by the fact that Mr. Kim obviously came from money and had a thriving investment counseling practice. They had wanted to vote against him simply because he was wealthy. But they loved the children.

"That one was for you, Mr. Perliss." I looked at Rodrigo through the glass window in the attorney visiting room of the jail as he described the $12,000 baby grand piano he had hidden in a storage unit. Rodrigo had purchased the piano with a forged check. I have represented Rodrigo since he was fifteen years old, mostly for burglaries of luxury homes in the posh neighborhood of Palos Verdes Estates, California. He had been in and out of Juvenile Hall for several years. Now as an adult, he discovered Internet fraud. He was buying expensive luxury goods using forged cashier checks. An undercover FBI agent, acting as a UPS driver, delivered a large package, and then followed him to the storage unit housing dozens of musical instruments, stereos, big screen TVs, computers and other assorted items, hundreds of thousands of dollars in stolen merchandise. I watched Rodrigo as he grew up, discovering more and more sophisticated criminal schemes every year. I constantly urged him to use his talents for legitimate purposes. He would listen dreamily and then tell me he wanted to be a lawyer. One time he asked if I could give him a law book to study. I gave him a book about the Fourth Amendment, search and seizure law.

I thanked him for thinking of me, then told him receiving stolen property is a crime punishable by a maximum of three years in prison. Unlike him, I was not interested in risking my freedom for a piano. This wasn't the first time Rodrigo had thought of me. After we beat a burglary case, he brought me a Louis Vuitton briefcase, apologizing that he did not have enough money to pay my fee but wanted me to have this elegant gift. I knew Rodrigo's mother and father. They were loving but busy parents with no resources, and could not afford an attorney fee after the initial retainer on Rodrigo's first juvenile case. I had been representing Rodrigo *pro bono* for years now, never expecting a fee and was thankful for the expression of gratitude. I liked the briefcase and proudly used it until I read the police report in his next case. He was charged with using a counterfeit credit card to purchase Louis Vuitton products from a fancy San Francisco department store. I was disappointed but not surprised. I sent the briefcase back to the department store anonymously. The police report also told of the fruits of a search of Rodrigo's home. Apparently, among various designer name products, the police found a law book, which they speculated Rodrigo was using to advance his knowledge on how to avoid prosecution.

This time Rodrigo was in real trouble. Now an adult, he had amassed a long history of theft-related crimes, was on felony probation on several matters and was facing fifteen years of new charges involving dozens of counts of Internet fraud, forgery and theft. This was his end of the line. I packaged everything together and Rodrigo ended up with a five-year prison term, two and a half of which he had to serve.

Rodrigo is not the only client I have represented *pro bono.* I defended an elderly indigent woman charged with stealing food from a grocery store. She stuffed frozen meat into her purse, was arrested and confessed she took it because she was hungry. She was charged with commercial burglary. When I was a DA, we would never file such cases, particularly when the defendant or his or her children were hungry and needed food. I went to court and received a copy of the police report. I was angry the DA had actually filed the case. I went into a tirade against the DA's office when the judge asked me how my client pleaded. I said I was never going to plead her guilty. I told the judge that it was immoral to criminalize taking a small amount of food because one is hungry. Eventually, the charge was dropped.

* * * * * * * *

Ten years ago, the remarking of computer chips was a prevalent crime. The computer chip is the brain of the personal computer, performing the vital function of executing software instructions. The chips were sold on the open market, along with other computer components. These chips were etched with a trademark, the product number and the speed at which the chip processes information. For example, earlier chips were marked 266, then 350, 400, 450 and 500. The higher the speed of the chip, the more valuable it was on the open market. Criminal organizations would buy huge supplies of low speed chips, remove the legitimate mark and then remark the chip at a counterfeited higher speed. To the layperson's eye, the change would be unnoticeable. To experts, the counterfeiting was obvious. The remarked chips would be sold through brokers at below the market value.

I represented a string of clients, including Howard Tseng, who was part of an organization which remarked computer chips. I had represented Howard on a DUI case and won a dismissal. From then on, I would get calls from his friends and associates. The crime no longer exists as the computer chip industry has completely changed. In the 1990s and early 2000s, people made millions remarking chips and selling them. Commercial counterfeiting is both a state and federal crime. The bigger the case, the more likely it is prosecuted by the United States Attorney's Office in Federal Court. Howard had set up various locations in which he was remarking and warehousing chips. The delivery locations were often post office boxes.

Engineers had learned to drill the computer chips to remove their speed limit, making a slower chip faster. Sometimes such chips would burn out. Howard foolishly sent burnt out chips to Intel as RMAs (Returned Merchandise Authorizations) for a credit. When engineers at Intel examined these chips, they immediately detected the speed had been altered and the chips remarked. They came after Howard. Five of his colleagues were arrested, all of whom I had represented at one time or another. Howard was abroad in China visiting potential business associates, on the way to his native country, Singapore. While there is no extradition treaty between the United States and China, there is one between the U.S. and Singapore. Howard was arrested after landing at Singapore's Changi International Airport.

I was called by Howard's family seeking help. I had already been contacted by his friends in custody and had represented one of them at a bond hearing, so I was familiar with the case. Howard's family put me in touch with his Singapore extradition lawyers, Horatio Lu and Olson Fang. Horatio and I later became trusted friends and transacted business together in Chengdu, China. Horatio petitioned the Bar Association of Singapore to allow me the appropriate legal status to visit the client in jail. I flew to Singapore and met with the client and Horatio. We spent the week discussing the allegations and facts. Eventually, Howard was extradited back to the United States, where he was prosecuted in Federal Court for commercial counterfeiting. I had a conflict of interest since I had represented another client on the same case. I referred Howard to a different attorney.

* * * * * * * *

Hunter Ma was a developer in Southern California during the boom days of the mid-2000s. He was building upscale residential homes, some of which were in the most exclusive neighborhoods of the San Fernando Valley. As the economy changed and money became scarcer, buyers withdrew offers and Hunter had difficulty securing construction loans for some properties, already under construction. Hunter began pulling money off one project to complete the construction of a different project. Each property was a distinct partnership with separate investors. He was moving loaned money from one partnership account to another, money that was secured by the respective properties. When the market collapsed, he was left holding properties with no money in the designated accounts to pay for development. Investors were complaining about the loans taken out on the properties. They wanted proof the money was spent on their investment.

To make matters worse, Hunter borrowed on the properties by forging investors' names on trust deeds. The new lien holders were deeded a higher priority on the chain of title. In the event that the properties were foreclosed, they would receive money first, before the earlier investors. Hunter had been a successful developer and had never been in any trouble. When the bottom fell out of the housing market, he was left with choices he had never faced. Expecting the market to rebound and the properties to sell, Hunter felt confident investors would then reap handsome returns. But when there was no economic recovery, he lost everything. He could not prove the investors' money was spent on the appropriate developments.

Some of the victims went to the police. Hunter was arrested and charged with multiple counts of forgery, grand theft and false personation. In addition, he was charged with an enhancement, that in the commission of these crimes, the victims lost over one million dollars. His bail was set at a million dollars, the loss to the investors. He could not raise the bail, so getting him out of custody was impossible.

In my discussions with the DA, I showed her files from the developments Hunter had completed over the past ten years. There were at least thirty successful projects which had gone smoothly. All of these investors reaped huge profits when the properties sold. I argued that Hunter, an honest, hard-working businessman, made a series of bad decisions in an effort to save everybody's investment. While illegal, his acts were not motivated by greed, but instead by the desire to finish the developments and pay investors their returns. I showed the DA that all monies received as loans were used for construction. The DA was impressed by the prior successful developments and understood the problems with the economy. We talked about how Hunter would be able to make restitution. Hunter, a highly skilled and potentially valuable employee, had job offers waiting for him once the case was over. My goal was to get him out of jail to start making restitution payments. I came to an agreement with the DA that Hunter would be released pending trial and begin working on his restitution obligations. He was freed from custody, borrowed some money from a friend and started to pay down the balance of the restitution. We continued to fight the case. In the end, Hunter agreed to a fair disposition. He would be placed on three years of formal probation, pay all restitution and spend 1,000 hours of community service building homes for the impoverished.

Hunter recently told me that his three-year probation was successfully completed. He was extremely grateful.

* * * * * * * *

Armando was an older single man who has faced many difficulties in his life, including a nasty strike conviction for a serious felony, a sex offense. Armando went to state prison for a number of years for that crime. Since he has been out of prison for the last fifteen years, he has done well, never re-offending. A solitary man, he has worked as a forklift driver.

One day, he was contacted via the Internet by a mysterious woman from Africa looking to meet men. She sent photographs of herself and they started corresponding regularly. She soon told Armando that she had fallen in love with him and wanted to come to America. She said she had access to money, but because of her peculiar financial situation, it was impossible to retrieve that money.

Usually when a relatively sophisticated person sees such e-mails, he or she recognizes the scam immediately. Armando had a funny suspicion in the back of his mind, but he was smitten by the enticing pictures of a stylish woman and the complimenting words she had written. Armando wanted to believe her. The woman wrote she would send a check, which he should deposit into his account. Then Armando could send her the funds, enabling her to withdraw her money in Africa and come to America. She sent him a third-party check which he took to the bank. He was a little suspicious so he planned to ask the bank officials if the check was legitimate. He approached the teller, mentioned something about the check and handed it to her. The teller told him to wait while she asked her manager. Armando later said he asked the teller if the check was any good. The teller later admitted that Armando had asked her some questions about the check, but did not recall the specifics. When the manager examined the check, he determined it was a forgery and contacted the police. The police came and arrested Armando. He was charged with felony forgery. Forgery is often misunderstood; it is not only the actual process of forging a name, but also the "uttering" of a forged check. If one negotiates a forged check, he or she is equally guilty of forgery. Armando was charged with felony commercial burglary (California Penal Code Section 459) and forgery (California Penal Code Section 470). Burglary is the entering of a location with the intent to commit a crime.

Armando had a major problem, his prior strike. The maximum punishment without the strike was three years, eight months in prison. Adding the prior strike doubles the term, so he was facing over seven years. In addition, a strike changes the custody credits against one's sentence. In most cases, including forgery and commercial burglary, an inmate gets an additional day credit for each custodial day, so one actually serves half his sentence. The strike changes half time in prison to eighty percent, so the consequences for Armando were severe.

Armando kept his entire file of e-mails and pictures from the Internet conversations with his girlfriend. In the early e-mails, he was told, "I'm a truthful and honest lady. I have impeccable Christian qualities." Soon, it was, "I love you so much and I want to give you my heart and soul." After Armando was scammed, he e-mailed his girlfriend that he was angry and was going to jail because of her. He asked for her address and phone number, which he never received. Most likely "she" was a muscular, athletic Nigerian man sitting in an Internet sweatshop, sending out thousands of emails. These scams are a large revenue source in Nigeria. Armando used a Public Defender for a while. The DA had offered thirty-two months in prison, at eighty percent. Armando was an older man now and feared returning to prison.

Although suspicious, Armando did not know the check was actually fake and thought he had done everything properly.

He hired me when the case was set for trial. I substituted in on the case and began to represent him. I reviewed the police reports and his file of pictures and e-mails. I researched and found an expert on Nigerian Fraud Schemes, a former FBI fraud investigator. The expert wrote a report after reviewing the discovery. He talked about the nature of Nigerian frauds, saying one in a thousand naive Americans, like Armando, fall victim. The expert wrote that the FBI would never seek a prosecution of such a victim. I learned that even a congressman was cheated by this scam. Some Christian ministers were lured by the promise of thirty million dollars for their church. The U.S. Postal Office reports about six million counterfeit letters from Nigeria each year.

Nigeria is a country with a population of 155,000,000, an excellent school system and few jobs. The Nigerian government usually turns a blind eye to these schemes. Such scammers use telephone books and e-mail extraction machines to get addresses. They often work from Internet cafes. Some, who are successful, have become local celebrities. They are heroes based on their success at defrauding United States citizens. America's naive fools are known as *mugus*. The *mugus* are motivated by greed and sometimes by wanting to help needy people. One lady was contacted by a "wealthy" Nigerian businessman who supposedly had a logging truck accident. He needed to use a foreign bank account to transfer money from Nigeria to a bank in Amsterdam and then to the United States where he would undergo reconstructive surgery. The lady sent him $10,000 to cover international banking fees and later was scammed even more, totaling $50,000. She said, "He sounded so sincere." Her motivation was to help him pay for surgery and earn extra money as a reward. Some victims of the scam have received a letter from the Nigerian Bureau of Restitution. These victims are told they will be sent one million dollars in restitution from the Nigerian government. They are asked to send $4,000 to cover the logistical costs. There's no such bureau.

I sent the expert's report to the DA who declared, "This is the District Attorney's Office, not the FBI." The DA said they would file on anyone they believed had committed a crime. They would continue to prosecute Armando, whether or not he had the support of a former FBI agent. I demanded a jury trial on Armando's behalf and declared ready for trial. The case was postponed for a few weeks to find an open courtroom. As I was leaving, I noticed the DA, when asked to describe the case, used the term, "Nigerian Fraud Case." Upon hearing that, I knew I had succeeded in changing the context from a serious strike offender committing a new felony to a lonely man getting tricked in a Nigerian Fraud Scheme.

The trial was delayed. Finally, the DA escorted me into his office and introduced me to his supervisor, the Head Deputy, who asked what I wanted for my client. I told him I expected a dismissal for this victim of a Nigerian Fraud. The Head Deputy said, if convicted, Armando would spend a long time in prison due to his strike. I said he was not getting convicted. The Head Deputy was clear about not dismissing the case and asked for a suggestion of a possible settlement. I thought out loud: "If he pleaded no contest a misdemeanor, with no jail or fines and a year of informal probation, I could petition to dismiss the conviction at the end of the year pursuant to 1203.4. If agreeable to the DA, I would propose it to my client." The Head Deputy said he would think it over. When I later returned to court, that was the offer. Armando considered the potential risks of a trial and the possibility of returning to state prison if he lost. He decided to accept the plea bargain. He pleaded no contest and twelve months later, we dismissed the case 1203.4.

Many Chinese immigrants are distrustful of government intrusion in their lives. In China, the less one tells the government the better, especially in matters of money. This causes a problem in the United States where reporting certain financial transactions is mandated. United States law requires all cash transactions in excess of ten thousand dollars be reported to the United States Treasury. Financial institutions, such as banks, are obligated to inform their customers of this registration requirement and to assist in the filing of a Currency Transaction Report. This report identifies the amount of the transaction, the name, address and occupation of the bank customer. Many new immigrants, fearing the loss of privacy, often try to evade this reporting requirement by breaking large deposits into multiple smaller transactions. For example, instead of depositing $15,000 into a bank, the customer deposits $8,000 in one transaction and shortly after, $7,000 in another, thus avoiding the need to file the appropriate transaction report. This structuring of deposits is illegal. Structuring is a federal crime and may be punishable by prison depending largely on the quantity of transactions and the total amount of money structured.

Attorney Max Tu referred Jackie Huang to me after Jackie appeared in his office regarding a confidential legal matter. When Max learned of the federal criminal investigation into Jackie's banking practices, he immediately sent her to my office. Jackie was a procurement clerk for a government agency and had been suspected of taking kickbacks from vendors. The FBI could not prove the kickbacks actually occurred, but did have proof of two nine thousand, nine hundred dollar deposits into the same bank account within three days. Their investigation revealed the two deposits were the result of the sale of Jackie's car, paid in cash on the date of the first bank deposit. Jackie had divided the money, which she deposited separately to avoid the registration requirement. The Grand Jury returned an indictment charging her with structuring. Jackie received a probationary sentence and a fine.

Sometimes new immigrants are misinformed. In one structuring investigation, a naive client was taught that depositing cash in excess of $10,000 is money laundering, and as a consequence, she always divided deposits into smaller amounts. She believed this was the law and had been doing so for years to "avoid the crime of money laundering." I explained to the authorities the client's innocent misinterpretation motivating her deposits. She was advised to cease such activities immediately. Law enforcement monitored her banking habits for the next year and when they found no new violations, luckily they left her alone. Not all suspects are so fortunate. Usually, ignorance of the law is no excuse.

* * * * * * * *

In the immigrant communities, commercial counterfeiting is found in varying forms. I have defended clients charged with counterfeiting sunglasses, purses, Rolex watches, Microsoft products and the like. One potential client was arrested at Los Angeles International Airport, entering the United States with 5,000 counterfeit Rolex watch faces. As an arriving alien, he asserted a political asylum claim and was detained pending his immigration hearing, then deported. He was never prosecuted for the counterfeit merchandise.

My client, Jackson Thi, was arrested for counterfeiting DVDs. He had a retail shop in Rosemead, a small storefront where he sold movies. He possessed five thousand counterfeit DVDs, found during the execution of a search warrant at his business. He was buying from China as well as burning DVDs himself. He would put the DVDs in cases, covered with plagiarized artwork. Then he would sell them. The Motion Picture Association of America (MPAA) often sends undercover agents in sting operations to purchase pirated movies. An agent appeared in Jackson's store and bought counterfeit DVDs. This purchase laid the basis for the search warrant. He was charged with multiple counts of piracy, punishable by state imprisonment. This was Jackson's first arrest.

One can visit shops in China or in the American Chinese community and often find counterfeit DVDs. When I stayed in Chengdu, China, it seemed every other store sold counterfeit movies. Pirating movies in China is not legal, but the law is rarely enforced. Government officials in China usually will not take action against DVD counterfeiters. Every now and then, complaints are voiced by the United States, other developed countries, the United Nations or the World Trade Organization. China might put on a show where they shut down a major counterfeit ring. A few days later, there will be new operators manufacturing and selling counterfeit products from the same factory. Chinese immigrants, like Jackson, do not usually take to heart the seriousness of the offense in America.

Jackson hired me to represent him. We were trying to work out a reasonable resolution and avoid a state prison sentence when he was again arrested for the same crime. Jackson liked to make my life miserable. Now he had two separate cases pending in Los Angeles Superior Court. Both cases were felonies, penal code violations of commercial counterfeiting. In addition, Jackson had an enhancement that he committed the second violation while out on bail. This enhancement added to the severity of the possible punishment, requiring that the two sentences run consecutively, plus two years. I had many discussions with the District Attorney's office. I tried to explain that my client, being Chinese, did not recognize the gravity of the conduct. I tried desperately to keep him from going to state prison. We resolved both cases for a probationary sentence, which included, as a condition of probation, one year in the county jail, which my client served by electronic confinement, house arrest. Jackson was ordered to pay the Motion Picture Association of America substantial funds in restitution. Happy to do so, he was grateful I kept him out of prison.

Jackson had the opportunity to thank me when my wife and I hosted Solomon Rose's family visiting from back East. We took them to an authentic Chinese restaurant in Monterey Park. The restaurant was elegant in its décor, with mahogany hardwood floors, Ming Dynasty landscapes hanging on the walls and a large revolving, finely-etched tray in the middle of each table. We were feasting on a delicious dinner when Solomon's brother nudged me, "Some guy over there is gesturing to you." It was Jackson Thi, sitting with a large group of influential looking friends. I said he was a friend of mine. Solomon knew me well enough to guess the true nature of the attorney client relationship. Solomon's mother mentioned that he looked important, as he was dressed in a regal double-breasted black suit. I exchanged a glance and a wave with Jackson. At the end of dinner, I asked for the check. The manager whispered, "The gentleman at the corner table has already taken care of it." Solomon, his brother and mother were impressed. Knowing I was a criminal defense lawyer, they speculated Jackson was some type of Chinese mobster.

* * * * * * * *

I represented Jimmy Vuong in state court where he was charged with selling controlled substances without a prescription, in violation of California Business and Professions Code Section 4060. United States Food and Drug Administration (FDA) investigators had received a tip that Jimmy was advertising prescription drugs in the Vietnamese newspapers. In a search of Jimmy's home, the FDA seized hundreds of plastic pill bottles and blister packs. Laboratory analysis of the seized drugs confirmed they were counterfeit, although they did not contain any controlled substances. As part of the investigation led by the FDA, local police had received an anonymous letter claiming Jimmy and an additional suspect had sold more than a million dollars' worth of Viagra over the last four years. According to the letter, Jimmy had advertised in a local Vietnamese newspaper with a contact number. The FDA was able to confirm the anonymous tip and obtained a copy of the ad from the Vietnamese newspaper. The ad offered "the best drugs manufactured in the U.S.A." It had instructions on how to use the drugs, "sold at the lowest prices in Los Angeles." The phone number listed was the same given in the anonymous letter. The District Attorney's Office prosecuting Jimmy in the Los Angeles County Superior Court case could not prove the pills actually contained a controlled substance, and failed to amend the complaint to allege counterfeiting. The case resulted in a dismissal after I pushed for Jimmy's right to a speedy trial on the allegation he possessed a controlled substance.

Several years later, Immigration and Customs Enforcement (ICE), in an unrelated investigation, learned of a large retailer of counterfeit Viagra tablets using a Vietnamese newspaper for advertisement. Their research led to the earlier FDA case and a second investigation against Jimmy was begun. This time surveillance, wire taps and undercover purchases were conducted, involving both FDA and ICE. The undercover purchases, recorded on videotape, started with a meeting between Jimmy and the buyer, and an introductory small purchase of ten blue tablets for the price of $100. At this meeting, the officer was advised that if he bought one hundred or more pills, he would only be charged five dollars per tablet. Thereafter, the undercover officer made five separate purchases of counterfeit Viagra from Jimmy. For each of those purchases, the undercover officer contacted the seller with the same phone number from the Vietnamese newspaper. Each time they would set up a meeting at a shopping center and the undercover officer would purchase blue, diamond-shaped tablets that resembled authentic Viagra. Subsequent forensic testing confirmed the tablets were counterfeit.

During this investigation, ICE learned of shipments of counterfeit Viagra labels originating from Vietnam. They also found Jimmy's Post Office Box. Investigators talked to an employee at the post office and learned that Jimmy had told her he was in the pill business. Often he would send packages to Vietnam from the post office. On one occasion, the postal employee contacted ICE and advised that Jimmy had dropped off packages for shipment to Vietnam. ICE officials obtained a search warrant for the packages. The warrant was served, the packages were opened and counterfeit Viagra was found inside. Investigators then set up large purchases of Viagra from Jimmy. Jimmy was arrested and indicted for conspiracy, trafficking in counterfeit goods and selling counterfeit drugs with intent to defraud and mislead. The federal indictment specifically alleged that Jimmy imported the raw ingredients and labels in separate shipments from Vietnam to his Post Office Box.

Then he manufactured the counterfeit Viagra pills with a tablet compacting press he kept at home. He sold the pills in the United States and Vietnam. Because I was successful in the first case, Jimmy hired me to represent him in the second. As a result of his prior case and the sheer volume of sales, coupled with the fact that Jimmy was not a U.S. citizen, the U.S. Attorney strenuously opposed his being released on bond. I made several motions in the United States District Court to set bond, but to no avail. Due to the fact that Jimmy had extensive business and personal ties in Vietnam, the Federal Magistrate feared Jimmy would flee if released. The potential for flight is the major issue when determining bond. Jimmy received a fourteen-month prison sentence.

* * * * * * * *

Often immigrant businessmen are unfamiliar with consumer protection rules, tax laws and corporate fiduciary duties in the United States and conduct business as if they were living in their home country. The five following cases illustrate this phenomenon. Traditional Chinese medicine includes the use of herbal products as health supplements. The herbal product Ping Xiao is widely sold in China as an immunotherapy treatment and cancer cure. Ping Xiao's advertisements claim the herbal compound fights off infection or disease by helping the immune system identify and destroy cancer cells or slow the growth of cancer in the human body.

Bin Qiang imported Ping Xiao in its raw herbal form into the United States. He then processed and packaged the final product for sale, shipping most of it back to wholesalers in China with a "Made in America" stamp. In order to maximize profits, Bin developed a website, selling the finished product in America through the website as well as in local Chinese language newspapers. The unsubstantiated claims of Ping Xiao as a cancer cure classified this substance as an unapproved drug and in violation of the California Health and Safety Code.

In addition to selling the product through online and phone-in purchases, Bin opened a sales office in his warehouse, where customers came to purchase the product, usually in a four to six week course of treatment, costing $1,000. District Attorney Investigators armed with warrants searched the warehouse and Bin's home, confiscating the product and the sales records. Fearing an imminent arrest, Bin hired me. I contacted the DA in charge of the investigation and scheduled a meeting; we discussed the accusations, the products and the seized records. The DA listed the crimes she believed were committed, including the least serious, false advertising. I told her I believed the case more resembled a civil matter and civil injunctions would ensure no further such violations. We had a number of meetings and finally came to an agreement on the case. The DA would not file criminal charges. My client would stipulate to a civil order enjoining him from conducting any more business involving Ping Xiao, terminate his various companies, pay fines and the costs of investigation, and not engage in the sale of any health supplement products. Bin dodged a bullet.

On another product-related false advertising case, I represented a restaurant supplier of frozen poultry. Buyers of the client's products complained to city officials that the actual weight of the frozen poultry fell one-third short of that listed on the box, in violation of the California Business and Professions Code. City code enforcement officials toured my client's warehouse and weighed the boxes. The total weight of the boxes matched the weight written on the label. When one of the boxes was opened, the code enforcement officers found the poultry packaged in large quantities of ice to ensure the product did not spoil. The weight of the ice was one-third the total weight listed on the box. The actual net weight of the poultry was only two-thirds of the stated weight. The client and his company were charged with misdemeanor false advertising. After the client hired me, I immediately sent letters to the client's suppliers demanding accurate labels on all packages purchased by the client. I appeared in court, showed copies of the letters to the prosecutor and argued my client was unaware of the mislabeling which occurred at the factory in China. The prosecutor asserted the crime was strict liability, that my client was guilty simply by virtue of placing the mislabeled products into the stream of commerce, despite his lack of knowledge. After several hearings, the case resolved as an infraction, a minor violation.

Gabriel Nguyen, a different client, was working in the Chinatown convenience store he and his wife owned for the previous ten years, when Los Angeles Sheriff Deputies seized fifty boxes containing one thousand counterfeit cartons of cigarettes. The nature of the cigarettes and the fact that state taxes had been avoided was not the purpose of the search and seizure, although eventually such charges were filed. The stated purpose of the raid was to protect the consumers who were purchasing cigarettes with unknown and potentially added dangerous chemicals. During the search, Gabriel admitted to knowingly selling the counterfeit cigarettes. He received a misdemeanor conviction, probation and substantial fines, but no jail time.

In China, fireworks are a common household item on hand for celebratory occasions. Having explosives is an illegal act in California. The California Penal Code defines explosives as any substance or combination of substances, the primary purpose of which is detonation and combustion. This includes many fireworks. Eugene Cheung was charged with possessing huge quantities of explosives, and since he had children in the home, with child endangerment. Police found a ton of fireworks in the house. The police were acting on a tip when they entered his Los Angeles County home. They confiscated eighty cases of illegal fireworks, valued at over $100,000. Fire department officials commented, "Had these fireworks exploded, half a city block or at least the house and the two houses on each side would crumble." This is a crime often punishable by state imprisonment because of the dangerous nature of the explosive material. I fortunately worked out a settlement for Eugene where he did not have to suffer a term of incarceration.

Patrick Chen and his wife had an ongoing import export business for a number of years. Patrick had started the company and then later sold a portion to his wife. His job was to market the business; his wife's to manage it. Most of those close to them knew their history and the couple's respective duties. The name of the corporation included Patrick's first name. He had a falling out with the wife, who left him. The wife filed a civil lawsuit trying to take the company, claiming she was the sole owner. Patrick fought the lawsuit. Both still had a claim to the business and the matter was pending in the civil courts. Since the wife tried to oust him from ownership, he started a new company. He moved some product to his new location. The wife accused him of theft and had him arrested, despite his protests. He was charged with felony theft and hired me.

I obtained the original Articles of Incorporation and bylaws. Patrick found a copy of the contract he had signed with his wife, which sold her a percentage as a shareholder. I went to court and fought the case, calling a half dozen witnesses who all testified Patrick was the owner and president. They all had dealings with him. I showed copies of the contract and incorporation documents to the DA. My client admittedly took the product, but they were his to take. One cannot steal from a company one owns. No crime was committed. The DA agreed and dismissed the case.

Chapter VII

Growing & Evolving: Merging Criminal and Immigration Law

It is not the strongest of the species that survive, nor the most intelligent, but the one most responsive to change.
– Charles Darwin

In 1996, the Illegal Immigration and Immigrant Responsibility Act (IIRIRA) was signed into law. This major shift in U.S. policy tightened immigration controls considerably. After IIRIRA, an alien, unlawfully present in the United States for a period of six months, who returns to his or her country, is barred from re-entering the U.S. for three years. If unlawfully present for twelve months, a ten-year bar now applies. IIRIRA also increased the classes of felonies for which non-citizens can be deported. The definition of an aggravated felony previously only included murder and trafficking of firearms. IIRIRA expanded the definition to include many other crimes. Specified crimes with sentences of one year or more incarceration, and even certain misdemeanors when defendants are sentenced to a year in jail, would now be considered aggravated felonies. Some suspended sentences might also be classified as aggravated felonies, requiring deportation. A defendant who commits a certain crime, and is sentenced to 365 days in jail is removed (formerly called "deported"), while a different person who commits the same crime sentenced to 364 days in jail is not. Thefts of $10,000 or more require removal, while thefts of $9,999 mean no removal.

When this law passed, it was incumbent upon every criminal defense attorney to learn the current changes in immigration law. Under the new law, what happens in criminal court, determines what happens in immigration court. In other words, the question of whether a non-citizen would be deported is already answered by the criminal lawyer's resolution of the case in the criminal courtroom. The sentence on the criminal case would seal the non-citizen's fate when it came to removal.

An example of having to work around immigration removal problems occurred in a credit card fraud case I handled in Long Beach Court. There is a large credit card fraud organization doing business in the immigrant communities. This organization steals credit card numbers assigned to cardholders throughout the world. They utilize existing cardholders' information and manufacture new cards with correct numbers, but different names. The new name would be the same as the buyer's, using a fraudulent ID, such as a driver's license. The buyer would purchase products, later to be returned, fenced or sold on E-bay or wherever such ill-gotten goods could be sold. In collecting the credit card information, a department store cashier or restaurant waiter would use a device known as a scanner, capturing legitimate credit card numbers. When a customer finished his or her meal and presented the credit card, a complicit waiter would scan the card before swiping it in the credit card machine. The scanner would collect thousands of credit card numbers to be given to that arm of the criminal organization responsible for making new cards. I have represented many defendants arrested for purchasing goods using fraudulent credit cards.

One of my clients, Mr. Henry Kong, was detained at a local department store after attempting to purchase items using a phony credit card in his name. He was arrested at the scene and charged with multiple counts, including felony commercial burglary (California Penal Code Section 459), attempted grand theft (California Penal Code Section 664/487(a)) and credit card fraud (California Penal Code Section 484(g)). Mr. Kong hired me to defend him on the charges. I had difficulty with the DA, who would not offer any reasonable disposition. She demanded six months in the county jail for this first time offender. A preliminary hearing occurred and I cross-examined the witnesses. At the end of the preliminary hearing, the judge held Mr. Kong to answer to the charges and set the case for a new arraignment in a different Superior Court Department.

I happened to know the DA in that courtroom. I talked to him about the impending case. He indicated a very reasonable disposition of probation with thirty days of community labor, such as picking up trash on the freeway or in a park, in exchange for a guilty plea on two of the charges. I told Henry, a lawful permanent resident, it was a good disposition as it kept him out of jail and we could later reduce the charge to a misdemeanor and dismiss it 1203.4. However, I feared Immigration might deport him. I had learned through my experience practicing immigration law that having two convictions of moral turpitude could result in the loss of the green card and removal from the United States. I went back and talked to the prosecutor explaining my concerns. He was unmoved by my argument. Prosecutors will often tell me that America would be better off without these criminals anyway. I suggested an alternative resolution to Henry. "Since you do not have to go to jail, why not offer doing more community labor in exchange for dismissing one of the counts?" Trying this approach, I added fifteen days to the community labor and went back to the DA to present my proposal. He agreed. My client completed his probationary terms. Thereafter, the case was reduced to a misdemeanor and dismissed. He had no problems with the US Immigration authorities.

There is an innovative form of justice called "restorative justice" or "reparative justice" that has emerged in different countries, including the United States. Restorative justice requires the offender take full responsibility for his or her actions. The offender "makes up for" and repairs, as much as possible, the harm caused, restoring some right to the wronged person. This might be accomplished by returning stolen goods or money, apologizing and dialoguing with the victim, and/or doing community service. In Longmont, Colorado, restorative justice is used instead of the court system for juvenile crime, where it is reported that nine of ten offenders complete agreements and charges are dropped. For serious crimes, both restorative and punitive justice might be applied. "People respond to crime by saying, 'Lock 'em up!'" says Professor Scott Wood, director of the Center for Restorative Justice at Loyola Law School in Los Angeles. "Offenders go to prison and learn to do even more terrible things," Wood explains. "Restorative justice lets them accept responsibility for what they did and become a better person."

Restorative justice sometimes applies in the resolution of minor crimes. One of my clients was arrested with five ecstasy tablets in his sock and charged with misdemeanor possession. His case was resolved after the client wrote a five-page essay on the health problems associated with drug abuse. Another client, a student, stole a valuable reference book from a school library. I contacted the City Attorney's Office prior to a criminal filing and offered a resolution involving the completion of forty hours of community service in lieu of the filing of a criminal complaint. They agreed. On a hit and run case, I tracked down the victim and offered to compensate his losses by way of civil compromise. I submitted the signed civil compromise forms to both the detective and the prosecutor's office, avoiding a criminal filing. On a case where my client was charged with marijuana possession and giving false information to the police, I persuaded the DA to accept five days of gardening in a local park in exchange for a dismissal. On a hashish possession charge my client went to fifteen Narcotics Anonymous meetings. The case was dismissed at arraignment.

* * * * * * * *

Immigration is the sincerest form of flattery.
– Jack Parr

Around the same time IIRAIRA took effect, I had numerous inquiries from potential clients in need of an attorney to minimize the impact of criminal convictions on their immigration cases, or to assist them in removal proceedings in Immigration Court. I had a basic understanding of the immigration laws and removal proceedings. I found that for every one client with a criminal case, I would be contacted by four or five potential clients with immigration problems. I attended seminars and learned the law and procedures to assist current and future clients with their immigration applications, petitions and appeals in Immigration Court.

Shanghai born, Anderson Bai, was now working for my law firm. As an immigration paralegal with a Master's degree in English from a U.S. university, he had been working in immigration law for many years. In addition to taking Immigration Court cases involving the consequences of criminal convictions, we began to extend our practice to other areas of immigration. This included family-based petitions for relatives of U.S. citizens, as well as employment-based petitions for multinational transfers, visas for specialty occupations, political asylum and investor visas.

In 1998, when Anderson started working with us, immigration from China was exploding. Having grown up in China with close relatives there, Anderson used his connections to set up appointments in Shanghai, Nanjing and Suzhou. We traveled to China and met with law firms and exit companies relative to United States visa applicants. The exit firms, which marketed their emigration services to Chinese nationals, needed foreign law firms to prepare and file their clients' visa applications. We prepared and signed cooperation agreements with twelve firms, detailing our fees for various visas.

Companies transferring multinational managers from China to their subsidiaries in the United States often had trouble with Immigration's approving these transfers. Sometimes Immigration would send a Notice of Intent to Deny an application, due to suspicions the parent company did not actually exist or had filed fraudulent documentation. We would travel to China to conduct overseas investigations to verify the authenticity of the companies. Then we would prepare a comprehensive report, including photos and documents to establish the legitimacy of the foreign corporation. In 1998 and 1999, we conducted several overseas investigations. We would videotape the operations and the workers, and interview the principals and employees about the nature of the business and the identities of the managers who were running the operations. We would prepare not only written reports, but often a video report, showing how the Immigration officials' assessment of the China-based company was mistaken. We were successful on these overseas investigations, which took us to Shantou, Shanghai, Shenzhen, Guangzhou, Chengdu and Keelong in Taiwan.

Ming Deng was a manager of the sales department of a China based import export subsidiary in Los Angeles. Prior to his admission to the United States as an L-1 Multinational Manager, he had served five years as head of the sales department of the parent company in Shanghai, China. He filed an application for a green card as a Multinational Manager Transferee and presented himself at the Immigration Office for an interview. During the interview, the Immigration Officer revealed that the US Consulate would conduct an overseas investigation to determine the legitimacy of the parent corporation. Ming was not concerned about this overseas investigation, as his parent company was well known and substantial. The documents submitted were authentic.

The Consulate's overseas investigation, however, erroneously concluded that Ming had not worked for the parent company as a sales manager. Ming learned this bad news from the authorities upon receiving the Notice of Intent to Deny his application. To qualify for this Multinational Manager Transferee green card, the beneficiary must have worked in a managerial position for at least one year within three years prior to filing the petition.

Ming had worked for five years before he was transferred to the U.S. subsidiary.

Anderson and I traveled to Shanghai and conducted our own overseas investigation. We visited the parent company located in a huge compound of multiple spacious buildings. Next to the workers' dormitory was the factory, by far the largest building in the compound as it housed hundreds of workers fabricating Chinese redwood furniture. Clouds of sawdust hung thick in the air commingling with toxic odors of industrial glues and adhesives, choking Anderson and me as we inspected the building. The workers seemed unaffected as they artistically and expertly toiled at their duties: sawing, carving, gluing and lacquering the products. They spent all day in this factory breathing in these poisonous fumes. I asked the production manager why the workers were not wearing protective dust masks to filter out the pollution. He replied that every month he gives each worker 30 masks, one for each day. Instead of wearing the masks, the workers sell them. In responding to my comments about the artistry of the workers, he said the company hires its employees from the same town in central China where woodworking is taught from generation to generation. I interviewed about twenty employees who confirmed Ming's service as sales manager for the five years preceding his transfer to the subsidiary in Los Angeles. I prepared declarations from these employees, took photographs and videotaped the company, as well as those who gave the declarations.

From Shanghai, we went to Keelong, Taiwan and conducted a similar investigation for a different client, a manufacturer of kitchen utensils. Within a week of returning to the United States, we prepared the paperwork and filed an appeal to Immigration relative to the Notice of Intent to Deny the green card applications. In one month, Ming's application was approved. Two months later, the Taiwanese client's application was also granted.

In addition to these lengthy overseas investigations, our job included more mundane cases, such as the typical filing of a green card petition for a spouse or a child, "family-based" cases. U.S. citizens would apply for their non-citizen family members to obtain green cards and eventually become citizens as well.

During an icy cold November, Anderson and I went to Shenyang in Northeastern China, where we met with clients applying for visas at the United States Consulate. Our goal was to prepare them for the visa interview. We met with one client who took us to a banquet. During the four years prior to this trip, my wife, Jia-Ning, had spoken Chinese to me at every opportunity. Anderson could not believe that after consuming Chinese whiskey at the banquet, I spoke Chinese effortlessly. All of our hosts were impressed. Without the encouragement of such spirits, I am not so fluent.

We also handled investor visas, commonly known as EB-5 cases, involving the capital investment of $1,000,000 into an "at risk" enterprise in the United States which creates ten full-time jobs. The investment could be reduced to $500,000 if the enterprise is located in a high unemployment area, defined as an area with an unemployment rate of one and a half times the national average. Under the investment visa category, the immigrant who invests into his own "at risk" enterprise would be required to have an active role in the management of the business. This created a problem for potential immigrants, unsure of their competency to run a company in the United States, having never done so before and not being able to speak the language. One alternative to this requirement was found in the law establishing a program of "regional centers." Utilizing a regional center, the investor could join a limited partnership, which uses an economic multiplier calculation to prove that ten full-time jobs would be created indirectly. Doing an EB-5 this way relieved the investor of having to participate in the daily operations of the enterprise. Often my job is to advise the client of the varied options in going forward with his or her entrepreneurial goals to obtain permanent residency in the United States. The only problem is the expense. These businesses are major undertakings. And while I was now working in immigration law, as well as criminal law, I found an overlap. Business consultants were cheating immigrants by hiring their own families as the ten employees and running the companies into the ground. The million dollar investment would be lost long before the EB-5 status would be granted. We handled our share of civil lawsuits alleging these frauds on behalf of our immigrant clients. The immigrant community must be very careful in America, where freedoms are sometimes used by people with ulterior motives.

* * * * * * * *

While many of our clients hired us on routine immigration matters, we also welcomed the challenge of complex and unusual cases. A Chinese woman who had twice married U.S. citizens lost the chance to gain permanent residency due to the sad and untimely death of both husbands during the pendency of the respective immigration proceedings. Ms. Stacey Liu's first husband was killed in a car accident in 1990, five days before their green card interview. Their green card application was based on his employment. Though Ms. Liu and her son appeared at the interview scheduled for the whole family, the death of the principal caused the denial of the green card.

Several years later, Ms. Liu married her second husband, who filed an immigration petition for her, but passed away prior to the interview. The couple was married only fifteen months, nine months shy of the required two years to qualify for a widow's exception. After visiting many law firms, none of which were willing to take her case, she came to us. Since her second husband had been a decorated veteran of World War II and a public servant, we believed that Congress might consider passing a private immigration bill. I contacted the local congressman and explained the situation, asking if he would sponsor such a bill for Ms. Liu. The congressman asked us to prepare Form I-360 Petition for Widow of United States Citizen, even though the couple had not been married long enough. He said he would submit our package and a private immigration bill when Congress was in session. Following his instructions, we prepared the required documents and submitted the I-360 petition to his office. Consistent with Ms. Liu's luck, while the bill was pending, the congressman was defeated in the next election. I tried the same approach with the new congresswoman who replaced him. She was not so sympathetic.

Time passed and there was no progress, so we decided to file the petition directly with Immigration, despite the client not meeting the requirements. Immigration set the matter for an interview. I attended the interview and explained the hapless circumstances of Ms. Liu's marriage history. I emphasized her second husband's contributions to the U.S. government and the private bill in Congress. I related how she had many equities in her favor, although her marriage did not last long enough for the technical requirements of the law. After hearing the story, the Immigration Officer granted her petition.

* * * * * * * *

Chinese people have a custom of giving gifts of red envelopes, containing varying amounts of money, to children on holidays or upon meeting friends, relatives and associates. Elderly Chinese will often carry a supply of red envelopes to have one available if the need arises. This is a tradition of generosity. The child who receives the gift has some money, but more importantly, has the feeling that he or she is special. The giver of the red envelope believes the gift represents good luck for him and the recipient.

In the year 2000, Mr. Long Fan entered the United States Consulate in Guangzhou and submitted an application for a visa to visit his daughter in the United States. When he presented the visa application, a small red envelope from inside his briefcase was accidentally enfolded in the pages of his passport. There were twenty Hong Kong dollars in that red envelope. The consular officer denied the visa believing the applicant had attempted to bribe her. For the next three years, due to his record of "attempted bribery" at the Consulate, each succeeding visa application was rejected. His U.S. citizen daughter, frustrated that her father could not come to visit the family in the United States, hired me. We sent a letter to the Consul General in Guangzhou, explaining the mistake and criticizing the consulate for denying the seventy-four year old applicant's visa request, keeping him from his family for so many years. In the letter, I asked the simple but obvious question, "Who would attempt to bribe a U.S. visa officer for the equivalent of two and a half U.S. dollars?" The client's visa was approved.

* * * * * * * *

I received a call from Jonathan Feldman, an Orange County medical malpractice lawyer and friend, referring me a client. As is often the case with Feldman, the referral is an unusual situation. This time the client, an American, had visa problems entering a foreign country. Bernard Manfield was a prolific travel writer whose business took him all over the world. He never had any visa problems entering foreign countries. On this occasion, the Costa Rican authorities refused his entry, having discovered that, as a young man, Bernard had been convicted of a petty crime, an event he had long ago forgotten.

I met Bernard and his pregnant wife Gwen in Feldman's office. Interviewing them, I learned that Actor Mikey Manfield was Bernard's father. When I was a small child, my favorite TV show was *Mikey Manfield's Animal Cartoons.* Mikey was in his early thirties and would do outrageous comedic skits between the cartoon screenings. He would dress up as a horse, a cow, a gorilla, a grinning monkey. After a long career entertaining children, Mikey retired to an oceanfront home in Costa Rica.

I sent a request to the court for the record of Bernard's conviction, but having taken place so many years earlier, the records had long since been destroyed. Bernard's Department of Justice record included a notation of this very old conviction, but was silent as to the question of whether the conviction was a misdemeanor or felony. Since the court record no longer existed, there was no possible way to confirm what I already suspected, that the conviction had been a misdemeanor. I researched the foreign country's visa laws and learned Bernard was eligible for a special type of visa. I prepared a letter explaining Bernard's twenty-eight year old case and the fact there was no record of the proceedings. With no record available, I felt free to present Bernard's background in the best possible light. I also completed Bernard's application and brought him to the Costa

Rican Consulate, where he was interviewed and granted the visa.

Bernard needed the visa to visit his father, Mikey, who at the time was terminally ill. Mikey had not seen the couple since before Gwen was pregnant. It was important to Bernard that he and Gwen could visit his very sick father. Gwen wanted her father-in-law to share in the couple's happiness of soon having their first baby and Mikey's first grandchild.

Six months later, Jonathan and Barbara Feldman celebrated their 40th wedding anniversary at the Hyatt Regency Newport Beach. Jonathan has sent me clients throughout the years, and many of them were at the party. I was profoundly touched when Bernard and Gwen approached and told me, "Thanks to you, we were able to visit Dad. He was excited and proud to see Gwen pregnant with his grandchild." Before Mikey died, I was privileged to repay him for the laughter he had given me as a little boy.

* * * * * * * *

A fugitive from justice in one's home country is not necessarily safe in a host country where there is no extradition agreement. In an Immigration Court case I handled, my client was a fugitive from justice in Taiwan relative to an allegation of theft. Since no extradition agreement existed, Taiwan had no access to U.S. courts to demand the return of the fugitive. Instead, the United States Immigration and Naturalization Service attempted to deport Mr. Christopher Hsiao, my client.

Mr. Hsiao had been politically active in Taiwan. Taiwan's government in the 1980s and 90s was largely comprised of members of the Nationalist Party, known as the Kuomintang (KMT). From 1988 to 2000, the President of Taiwan was Lee

Teng-hui, leader of the Kuomintang. His Vice-President, Lien Chen, was a rival of politician James Soong. The two rivals led factions inside the Kuomintang Party. Mr. Hsiao was affiliated with one of these factions. When his faction lost a position in local government, Mr. Hsiao was not only out of a job, but accused of misconduct. The infighting in the party ultimately led to the disintegration of the party's majority. James Soong left the Kuomintang and started his own party, called the People's First Party. The separation caused the Kuomintang to lose the 2000 election to the Progressive Party led by Chen Shui-bian, now in prison for graft.

Mr. Hsiao had been responsible for the local party's treasury for several years. When his faction lost in the election, the new faction tried to disgrace their competitors, in order to eliminate them. They alleged criminal charges against the rival faction and my client. By the time the charges were leveled, Mr. Hsiao was living in the United States. The Immigration Service tried to strip Hsiao of his green card and have him deported to Taiwan. Mr. Hsiao hired me to represent him in these Immigration Court proceedings. I filed a brief explaining the entire political situation in Taiwan and how Mr. Hsiao had committed no crimes. He was the unfortunate victim of political rivalry. The judge insisted the Immigration Service prove the allegation, which they could not. My client, only a suspect, had not been convicted of any crimes in Taiwan. The Immigration Judge refused to revoke Mr. Hsiao's green card, agreeing with my argument that there is an extradition process in America that should be used in these situations. Since Taiwan and the United States do not have such an agreement, no such process could be used in this case. Taiwan is a vibrant democracy and democracies, like reasonable minds, can differ.

Chapter VIII

Lawyering & Loitering Abroad: Taiwan, Chengdu, Europe, Shanghai & Israel

Perhaps travel cannot prevent bigotry, but by demonstrating that all peoples cry, laugh, eat, worry, and die, it can introduce the idea that if we try and understand each other, we may even become friends.
– Maya Angelou

I came to respect Taiwan's flourishing culture and society when in 1993, my wife Jia-Ning and I spent time in her home city, Taipei. On my first trip to Asia, I arrived at Chiang Kai-shek International Airport, now called Taiwan Taoyuan Airport. My initial thought upon leaving the airport was how difficult driving was in this seemingly uncontrolled traffic maze. Jia-Ning was a pro, having grown up in Taipei. She had the use of a white Subaru, similar to many of the cars on the road. She took me for coffee at the Grand Hotel, at the

181

time considered one of the top ten hotels in the world. Foreign dignitaries often stay at this famous hotel overlooking Northern Taipei. The hotel was built in 1952, in the architectural style of an ancient Chinese building, with its tilted roof, red pillars and dragon motifs.

We toured Taiwan, enjoying the bustling night markets and the spectacular seafood restaurants. We enjoyed the nightlife, an Irish pub with a Canadian band and karaoke clubs where Jia-Ning sang Chinese and English songs. We watched the changing of the guard at the Veterans Memorial and visited the Chiang Kai-shek Memorial. We drove through intriguing small towns throughout Taiwan, many having their own indigenous specialized craft. One town, Sanyi, situated north of Taichung, was famous for its handcrafted wood sculptures. Another, Yinge, near Taipei, was renowned for porcelain art. Years later, our children enjoyed going to Yinge where they designed and crafted porcelain artwork themselves. We went to the town of Yehliu, overlooking the ocean, an area with unusual natural rock formations; some, like the famous "Queen's Head," resembled people or animals. We went to Keelong, a fishing city in the North, and had a delicious fish dinner. Jia-Ning taught me that it is bad fortune to turn over the fish, as such act symbolizes a capsized boat. We toured the National Palace Museum, which housed art and artifacts from thousands of years of Chinese history. The priceless pieces had come to Taiwan with Chiang Kai-shek when he and his forces withdrew from the mainland. During World War II, in order to protect the artworks from the invading Japanese, Chiang organized them into separate shipments. Throughout the war, the art and artifacts were regularly moved throughout China to avoid discovery by the Japanese. The shipments were separated so if one was confiscated, the others would be safe.

Halfway through the trip, I needed to visit the Taipei branch of the Bank of America to cash some traveler's checks. Jia-Ning dropped me at the curb in front of the bank. I cashed my traveler's checks, returned to the car and sat in the passenger seat. I looked over to Jia-Ning. A Chinese man was sitting there. He did not speak English and I did not speak Chinese. I smiled, apologized in the only language I could and left. Jia-Ning's car, immediately behind the one I had entered, was identical. She laughed hysterically as I sheepishly sat down, this time in the correct seat.

Jia-Ning and I went to the observation deck of Taiwan's tallest building at the time, the Shin Kong Tower. We looked down at the sparkling city lights of Taipei. In the year 2004, Building 101 was constructed in Taipei, dwarfing the Shin Kong Tower, and becoming the tallest skyscraper in the world. Its notoriety did not last long. Dubai's Burj Khalifa, completed in 2009 at a cost of 1.5 billion dollars, surpassed Building 101.

When I returned to Los Angeles, I took a course of study in conversational Chinese at UCLA. Since we have been married, Jia-Ning speaks to me in Chinese as much as possible. She would repeat the same Chinese commands daily, "Wake up, Take a shower, Brush your teeth, Eat breakfast, Go to work." After a while, I picked up a lot of Chinese. This was of great benefit when I later spent time in Chengdu, where I had to speak Chinese to eat, take a taxi and handle daily affairs. After our trip to Taiwan, we returned annually to visit Jia-Ning's family.

* * * * * * * *

All journeys have secret destinations of
which the traveler is unaware.
– Martin Buber

Our business in the Chinese community prospered. We were advertising extensively in the San Gabriel Valley. Because of my background as a former Deputy District Attorney, many Chinese were interested in hiring me. We employed Chinese speaking staff. My firm was doing civil and business cases, immigration cases and all areas of criminal defense.

I was approached by a friend, Xiaoling Zhu, who claimed she had *guanxi* with the Justice Minister of Sichuan, a hugely populated province in Central China. The Minister wanted an American firm to open a foreign representative law office. Xiaoling explained there were one hundred and three such foreign law firms in China, all located in the East (Beijing, Shanghai, Guangzhou and Shenzhen). Sichuan did not have a foreign representative law firm. In order to promote trade between the United States and Sichuan, I was told the Ministry of Justice sought a U.S. law firm. I learned that other U.S. law firms in China were among the largest firms in the world. I felt the Sichuan Justice Ministry would not be interested in my firm of just a couple of lawyers. Xiaoling maintained that, based on her strong connection, size did not matter.

I knew that U.S. law firms situated in China were representing American businesses. My goal, in contrast, was to market to Chinese intent on immigrating and/or doing business in the United States. I discussed it with my law partner and we decided to go through the application process. This required many documents and forms to be filled out, backgrounds and histories to be provided. It required an interview, so after the months it took to do all the paperwork, I scheduled a trip to Chengdu for the interview.

My partner and I met with the Minister of Justice and the President of the Bar Association. We stayed at the Crown Plaza Hotel, where I met several interpreters, one of whom, Amanda Xu, was introduced to me as the best English-speaking interpreter in Chengdu. Amanda became a friend of the family and visited us both in Los Angeles and later when we lived in Shanghai.

Our interview took place at the Sichuan Ministry of Justice in Chengdu. They seemed to like us and our answers. They particularly valued my background as a former prosecutor. They advised they would forward our application to the National Minister of Justice in Beijing. A year later, we received a fax congratulating us, advising that our petition had been granted.

Ten days later we were in Beijing attending the ceremony to receive our certificate. Eleven new foreign representative law offices were receiving their licenses. All but us were sizeable U.S. or European firms. During the ceremony, each firm's representative sat in tall chairs, thrones. It was a typical Chinese affair: lots to eat and plenty of alcohol to drink for the requisite toasts to the attending dignitaries. The National Minister of Justice started the festivities with a speech welcoming us to China. He turned over the microphone to one of the first American lawyers licensed in China, whose office was in Beijing. He was from a large law firm located in the Midwest; one of his partners was a former Vice-President of the United States. This blustery, arrogant attorney spoke endlessly about how he and the former Vice-President were such good friends. I leaned over to the European attorney sitting in the throne next to mine. He was from a two-hundred year old Belgian law firm. A little tipsy, I said, "On behalf of the people of the United States of America, I apologize to you for this pompous ass." He laughed heartily, nearly falling off his throne. We kept in contact and later on, he helped me with a case in Belgium.

* * * * * * *

A Cuban, a Frenchman, a Beijing man and a Sichuan man are seated together on a train. The Cuban takes a cigar from his pocket and tells the group, "Ahh, a Cuban cigar, the best in the world." He lights the cigar, takes two puffs and throws it out the window. "In Cuba," he says, "these wonderful cigars are a dime a dozen." The Frenchman opening a bottle of delicious French red wine, says, "Romanée Conti, the world's finest Burgundy." He takes a few sips and throws it out the window. "In France, such bottles are as common as Perrier water." All eyes focused on the man from Beijing who grabbed the Sichuan man and threw him out the window.

When I arrived in Chengdu as the foreign representative, I needed to obtain an Expert's Certificate, allowing me to stay in China beyond the short time usually allowed business travelers, and a Zed Visa for multiple entries. This involved applications at the local Public Security Bureau and a trip to the health department for a thorough physical examination. The physical was embarrassing as most of the staff were women doing a detailed examination: an EKG, chest x-rays and the probing of every part of my foreign Caucasian body.

We received our certificate and now had permission to open the Chengdu office. We negotiated a lease and purchased furniture, but we did not have staff. This was a difficult task, since our sphere of contacts was so small. In the past when looking for office workers, we would find candidates simply by getting the word out. We did not know sufficient people in Chengdu to communicate that we were a new company in town that needed a bilingual employee. I discovered a Chinese company called Fesco. Fesco was designed to assist foreign enterprises doing business in China in need of human resources. They started in Beijing in 1979 as a result of China's reform and opening to the world economy. Fesco charged a small fee to allow me to review ten resumes, which it kept in its databank of English-speaking office workers. I paid the fee and received the resumes, none of which were satisfactory. I continued to pay for more resumes but had little success. Finally, I asked Fesco's manager if I could use the entire data bank, sit at one of their computer stations and go through the resumes. He agreed. I went through hundreds of resumes, picking the twenty best. I interviewed them and ranked the top five. From those, the first choice told me she had just been hired by a large foreign firm in Chengdu. I hired Janie, my second choice and the best English speaker on my list. She helped organize our grand opening party at a large teahouse in Chengdu. We invited the Ministry of Justice, members of the bar association, as well as friends and acquaintances we had met to date. This event was covered in the local newspapers.

Three months later, Janie's application for immigration to Canada was approved. She surprised us, saying she was leaving the firm and moving to Canada. I went through the entire process again and hired a new secretary. Soon after opening our office, the local media requested a news conference. They wanted to introduce the new foreign law firm to the local community. The meeting was held in our Chengdu office conference room. There were five reporters, representing the four major newspapers and one small English language paper. I was astounded that the first question asked for a comment on the contrast between Chinese judges who seem to rule in favor of the highest bidder and American judges who are required to act according to the law. Chinese reporters were like their U.S. counterparts, attacking with the toughest question first. Bribery in China is a common everyday manner of conducting business, which would result in steep prison terms in the United States. I did not want to alienate any members of the government who had just given me a certificate to open a foreign law office in Chengdu. I was stuck. Having no personal knowledge of judicial bribery in China, I took the easy way out. I maintained an ignorant attitude. I said I give every judge the benefit of the doubt, hoping he would do his best to make the right decisions on cases that came before him. I told the reporters that I expect a judge, whether American or Chinese, to act in good faith. I left it at that.

One of the members of the U.S. Consulate in Chengdu had an attorney wife, a visiting professor at a Chengdu law school. She asked me to give a lecture to her class on American law. I prepared and gave a lecture in English. Surprisingly, the students understood me. Their English was excellent and their questions challenging.

We advertised in an English magazine in Chengdu called *Go West*, a great resource for expatriates living in Sichuan. They also published our name under "Services in Chengdu," which resulted in many calls, including an American man in his early sixties. He was an English teacher in a small village in Sichuan and had married a younger woman in her mid-thirties, also a teacher, whom he wished to immigrate to America. I met him in my Chengdu office where he told me his story. We signed a retainer agreement and my office prepared and filed the paperwork for him to immigrate his wife. I was concerned about the age difference, but he and his wife were very much in love. He wanted to bring her to America, which, fortunately, we were able to facilitate.

Jia-Ning's father was from Sichuan, and had many relatives in Chengdu. He had been trained as an air force pilot by the Kuomintang during the war against the communists in the 1940s. When the communists won, Chiang Kai-shek and his air force fled to Taiwan. My father-in-law was with Chiang's forces and left a large family in Sichuan.

After I opened the foreign representative law office, I needed an apartment. We rented a breezy garden apartment in the southern area of Chengdu. On one of my early trips, Jia-Ning joined me and together we furnished the apartment with modern furniture and drapes. We bought household items for daily use, the most important of which was a coffee maker. Jia-Ning has a talent for finding local places of interest for eating, shopping and culture.

On this trip, we stayed two weeks. It was a dreadful time for America. While we were there, New York's Twin Towers were destroyed in the largest terrorist attack in American history. On our Chengdu apartment television, I watched in disbelief and sadness as the Twin Towers disintegrated. It was surreal to be out of the country at this time. I called the United States Consulate in Chengdu to inquire of the situation in New York. Chicago born Visa Officer, Mort Altman, answered the phone. We talked and decided to meet for lunch the next day. In the following years, Mort and I became friends. We would make a point of getting together during my visits and one time, over Passover, he and I joined a Seder (Passover meal) at the home of several Israeli students studying Traditional Chinese Medicine at the local university. It was difficult for Jia-Ning and me to return home after 9/11, as many flights were cancelled for fear of terrorism. Everywhere we went, people would say, "You're an American. We're so sorry this happened. We love America."

Jia-Ning and I were moved by the outpouring of genuine sympathy.

Jia-Ning grew up in Taiwan and had never met her relatives in mainland China. During her youth, it was difficult for Taiwanese to visit the mainland. We were determined to meet these relatives who had always been a mystery. Her father had recently reunited with the China family, so we had their contact information. Wanting to introduce Jiai-Ning's family to American food, we decided to arrange an American style brunch at one of Chengdu's fanciest five star hotels, the Crown Plaza. Chengdu was not an expensive place. Even the fanciest Chinese restaurants were priced well below their American counterparts. American restaurants in Chengdu were in short supply, however, and accordingly expensive. I did not expect Jia-Ning to have such a large family. We spent a fortune and they hated the food. One of Jia-Ning's relatives, a colonel in the People's Liberation Army, poured two glasses of whiskey for me and one glass for himself. He proposed a toast to my new office and to American-Chinese friendship. He said, "America is twice as great as China so you have to drink two glasses of whiskey to my one." The next toast came from me. I toasted to China and Jia-Ning's glorious family with all their magnificent children. I poured three glasses of whiskey for him and one for myself.

"Since China has three times America's population, you must drink three." He laughed and drank.

* * * * * * * *

Jonathan Feldman often refers me atypical cases, this time a father who received word his daughter was incarcerated in Holland. Dad was worried and turned to Feldman, the only lawyer he knew. Two days later, the father was in my office. The client was being held in Holland on a fugitive extradition warrant emanating from Belgium. While in Holland, she attempted to leave the country and was arrested at Amsterdam's Schiphol Airport. She was transported to a jail in Terapel, Northern Holland, pending her extradition to Belgium. Within a week, I was on a flight to Belgium. Before leaving, I set up a meeting with the Belgian lawyer I had joked with in Beijing. He was a partner in a prestigious law firm. I advised him in advance that I had a case in Belgium and needed his help. He assigned a criminal lawyer to help me.

In Brussels, I walked from my hotel to the Palace of Justice to review the public file. The Palace of Justice was built in the 1700s. At the time, it was the largest building in Europe. Its tremendous size, shape and general appearance faintly resembled the U.S. Capitol Building, if unpainted and abandoned in a state of disrepair for centuries. This enormous building looked like it bypassed modern times, evoking visions of guillotines. It was nightmarish.

I went into the building, found the equivalent of a Clerk's Office, advised them I was an American attorney and asked to see the case file, which they cordially showed me. Upon my request, they copied all the reports. Since the reports were in Flemish, impossible for me to read, I hired a Flemish translator. In two days I had an English version of the file, complete with police reports and statements of witnesses. I made copies for the extradition lawyer in Holland and the Belgian attorney. The Belgian lawyer, a professor at one of his country's most prestigious law schools, and I went over the files in detail. The lawyer explained criminal procedure in Belgium. I told him I was next going to Amsterdam to hire the extradition lawyer to assist us with the extradition matter in Holland.

I left for Holland and met with the extradition attorney I had found before leaving Los Angeles. I gave her a copy of the police reports, and then drove to the jail in Terapel to visit the client. I spent that night in a charming Bed & Breakfast, across a wooded path from a large windmill. I had been to correctional facilities throughout the United States and knew the law and order nature of U.S. prisons. In Holland, it was very different. I was not accustomed to prison guards dressed in civilian clothing. They respectfully called the inmates "Sir" or "Madam." One guard asked if she could bring us some water and directed us to snack machines. I told her I was from America and had visited many prisons in my country, but never witnessed any prison like this. "You people are so courteous to the inmates." The guard smiled, "The prisoners' lives are difficult enough already. We do not need to make it any harder." I discussed the proceedings with my client, tried to make her feel at ease and told her I would see her in Belgium.

Before leaving Holland I had a night out. I was curious about Amsterdam's Red Light District. I walked around and observed small rooms with picture glass windows and women behind them. The women were dressed in theme clothing: librarians, nurses, businesswomen and cowgirls. It was an odd scene, unlike anything in the United States. There would be a side door to a little cubicle, where men could enter a back room. I stopped in a smoky nightclub where patrons were drinking heavily. I saw people from all over the world speaking English, German, French and Spanish. On the countertop of the bar, adjacent to where customers were sitting on stools, a naked woman was dancing erotically. She held a can of whipped cream in her hand and was spraying it over the front of her body. She would stop to accept tips from those who licked the whipped cream from her skin. I noticed she wore a small necklace, from which dangled a Star of David. I was mortified.

This was my first trip to Europe, and I could not resist the occasional thoughts of World War II and the Holocaust. This shocking and traumatic event weighed heavily on world Jewry in the decades that followed the war. Born in 1958, thirteen years after the war ended, and raised in a Jewish home in metropolitan Detroit, I had grown up with the stories of the Holocaust and had read *The Diary of Ann Frank* at a young age. Ann Frank was from this very city and the only person I had ever heard about from Amsterdam. Now, I was watching a woman dancing naked, wearing a Star of David, and debauched men publicly devouring whipped cream from her nude body. It was too much, sacrilegious. I went to her and said, "Why are you wearing a Star of David? You're not Jewish!"

"I am Jewish."

"I don't believe you're Jewish." I could hear German spoken by a group at a table behind me. I wondered what they thought of the naked Jewess dancing for them.

"It's good money."

"Does your mother know what you're doing?"

"No, Mom doesn't know."

"I don't believe you're Jewish." Indignant, she started speaking Hebrew to me.

The next day I left Holland for Belgium. After I reported back to the Belgian lawyer, we began preparations for the court proceedings. He did an outstanding job and my client was acquitted. The client spent a total of three months in European prisons. She was home on the ninety-first day.

* * * * * * * *

Chengdu is home to panda bears at Giant Panda Bear Park, ninety-two acres of natural habitat. I strolled along the well-trodden paths and watched the bears while caring for their cubs. In the evenings, I enjoyed Chengdu's hot pot spicy delicacies, and relaxed in teahouses, decorated with paintings and rock art, some with miniature gardens. While touring by boat in the neighboring city of Leshan, I rounded a bend and the largest stone-carved Buddha in the world appeared before me. It was a statue of Maitreya, a future Buddha, who it is said, will come to Earth to bring wisdom and compassion. The stone sculpture was a sitting monk, 233 feet tall, a large face with exaggerated ear lobes, hands resting on his knees. Its smallest toenail easily sat an average sized person. It was constructed during the Tang Dynasty due to the efforts of the monk, Hai Tong. After twenty years of begging, Hai Tong had enough money to begin the project. When local authorities tried to confiscate the money, he suddenly dug out his own eyeball. The horrified officials ran away. The carving, overseen by two of Hai Tong's disciples, took ninety years to complete. Chiang Kai-shek used Sichuan as his capital during World War II. His Kuomintang Party brought businesspeople, workers and academics to Chengdu. They founded many of the industries and cultural institutions, which continue to make Chengdu an important center. During the Chinese Civil War, Chengdu was the last city on the mainland to be held by the Kuomintang-controlled government. The People's Liberation Army took the city on December 10, 1949, and what remained of the Kuomintang government left for Taiwan.

Our Chengdu office was in a building called the Western Tower, which housed many of Chengdu's foreign businesses. It was located on the corner of Lingshiguan Lu and Renmin

Nan Lu, down the street from the United States Consulate, next door to Chengdu-located Worldwide Physician Services, a medical clinic catering to foreigners. In China, food-borne diseases are a major problem. Hospitals and clinics may not be as sanitary as their Western counterparts. There was a growth of these Western style clinics to care for sick Westerners traveling through China. Amanda Xu now worked for Worldwide Physician Services, one of its corporate officers being Jeremy Richards. Jeremy and I became friends. When I first met him, in addition to Worldwide Physician Services, he was also a principal in a huge mining company in Sichuan. Later, Jeremy opened a Western style nightclub in Chengdu. As I continued to visit Chengdu over the years, I would frequent his club, which became the primary meeting place of most Western foreigners in the Chengdu area. Jeremy's firm hired us on a civil matter in the United States.

When we met Jia-Ning's Chengdu family, one of her cousins was married to Zhen Long who spoke just enough English to communicate. He started hanging around us and would show up at my office. He wanted a job in our firm, but there was insufficient business at the time to justify hiring him. He was so persistent we hired him anyway. He had attended a local Chengdu law school and knew many of Chengdu's law firms. Though his English was limited, he helped us design the law firm's brochure and introduced and marketed us to other firms.

Zhen Long's English communication illustrates a typical problem American businessmen sometimes have with Chinese employees. Problems occur not only from language, but also as a result of cultural differences. In America, for example, when asking a question, we expect a direct answer.

When a yes or a no question is asked, a yes or no answer is anticipated. If an explanation is necessary, it would follow the yes or no. In Chinese, the explanation often comes before the yes or no answer. It is common that the answer would begin with the word "because." Then a twenty-minute story would follow. Zhen Long would take me through long, convoluted answers. I would have to listen to an entire story before I could hear an answer to my question. This is actually very helpful to Chinese defendants. When cross-examined by a prosecutor in court, the prosecutor cannot lead and argue with them. All the prosecutor can do is ask his questions, and then grudgingly hear the whole story. Zhen Long had done this to me for months and I complained to him constantly. "Just get to the point," I would say. I finally had enough. After a question and typical, prolonged response, I said, "Stop, Zhen Long, I just want a yes or a no." He could not comply. Finally, I said, "Zhen Long, you need to think about your job and whether or not you like it. I am going to ask you this question again. You have to answer yes or no, nothing else, just one of those two words. If you do not answer with one of those two words, you will need a new job." I asked again. He looked me in the eye, paused for a few moments and said, "Yes."

Zhen Long and I often talked about the problems obtaining visitor's visas to the United States. Because many Chinese visitors overstay their time restrictions, consular officers are reluctant to grant visas, particularly to young marriage-aged women and students applying to not so reputable schools. Because visa processing is so difficult, knowing visa officers at the various consulates is sometimes helpful.

Zhen Long and I discussed his visiting the U.S. for training in the Los Angeles office. I wrote an invitation letter and helped him fill out the visa application. The Chengdu Consulate called our Los Angeles office to confirm the truth of the letter. His application was approved and he came to the United States for three weeks. His training included basic U.S. law, particularly litigation proceedings. The discovery process in a lawsuit usually includes the answering of interrogatories and requests for admissions of facts. When such discovery requests are served on the parties, there is a deadline to answer the questions. Someone has to translate the questions and assist the client to write the answers accurately. This training was important to the firm since we were now getting more and more litigation cases from Chengdu. After the three weeks of training, Zhen Long returned home.

The next year, Zhen Long wanted to return to the U.S. for further training. We prepared another letter and Zhen went back to the consulate. The most important factor the consular officer considers in granting a visa is the applicant's past travel. Has the applicant previously been to the United States and returned to China within the period of his authorized stay? If so, the applicant is a good risk to return. Given his record of returning to China within his authorized visitation, Zhen Long's second visa application was approved immediately. Zhen Long left China for his second training session in the Los Angeles office. He never arrived for training. I never saw him again. Perhaps someday he will appear in my San Gabriel Valley office: "I'm here for my training."

* * * * * * * *

There is a vague popular belief that lawyers are necessarily dishonest. Let no young man choosing the law for a calling for a moment yield to that popular belief — resolve to be honest at all events; and if in your own judgment you cannot be an honest lawyer, resolve to be honest without being a lawyer.
– Abraham Lincoln

Sometimes a lawyer has to say frankly, "Don't hire me." While working in Chengdu, we experienced some rather uncommon legal situations, not ordinarily found in our U.S. offices. Unlike Shanghai and Beijing, Chengdu, in Western China, was just starting to blossom. It was reputed for its innocence and simplicity. A man came to my office, carrying with him what looked like an ancient document. He told us that it had been buried in caves since Chiang Kai-shek left China for Taiwan. He related the document was a $5,000,000 U.S. bond, which was given by the United States government to Chiang Kai-shek to help procure weapons to fight the communists. Chiang left for Taiwan before he had time to use the bond. Looking at the bond, I noticed it had been issued by the United States Ministry of Finance. When I pointed out the United States does not have a Ministry of Finance, but instead a Department of Treasury, the man said this was a CIA ploy to protect the bond from being negotiated should it fall into the wrong hands. In other words, if the enemy found it, they would think it was a fraud. I told him it really was a fraud. He did not believe me. The English spelling and grammar on the bond were incorrect. The man wanted me to negotiate the bond with the Department of Treasury. I laughed, saying it was illegal to even attempt to negotiate that obviously fake bond. It is a crime to negotiate a forged instrument.

He would not listen. He insisted on my taking the case. I tried to dissuade him from hiring me to negotiate the forged document, so I told him I would not do this based on a contingency fee. He would have to pay a prohibitively large sum in advance before I agreed to help him. Already knowing the result, I told him I could write the Treasury Department to request an opinion on whether a copy of this document was legitimate. He was happy that I would help him. Thinking it was an act of futility and not wanting to take his money for no reason, I googled the language of the document and found a United States Treasury website showing the exact bond and describing the same story the man told. Apparently, I was not the first lawyer with such a case. I showed him the picture of the bond on the website from the Treasury Department, which explained its clearly fraudulent nature. At this point, he understood and took my advice not to spend the money on a lawyer. In China, there are millions of similar stories. Another illustration follows.

I was asked by the CEO of a Chinese company to review a contract. A U.S. buyer wanted to invest twenty million dollars into this Chengdu company. The Chinese CEO was advised the American company was publicly traded on NASDAQ. I reviewed the contract the American company's "lawyer" had prepared. Under the agreement, the Chinese company had to pay a brokerage commission to a Hong Kong firm prior to the receipt of the twenty million dollars. The Hong Kong broker's fee amounted to $17,000, an obvious fraud. In my Los Angeles offices, such silly cases would be weeded out by my staff, long before they made it to me.

For every dozen frivolous cases, one gem appeared. A businessman came to the office and showed me a copy of a $250,000 arbitration award on a breach of contract matter. An

American company had defended the lawsuit and lost. Using the United Nations Convention for the Enforcement of Foreign Arbitration Awards, my Los Angeles office filed a petition in the United States District Court to confirm the award. Most international contracts between foreign companies and Chinese parties have arbitration clauses. The reason for these clauses is the credibility deficit of the Chinese judiciary. In contrast, the China arbitration organization, CIETAC, is highly reputable. It is staffed with arbitrators who are former judges from Hong Kong and other legally sophisticated jurisdictions. Their decisions are well thought out and reasoned. Their written opinions would impress any Western lawyer.

We researched how to enforce these foreign arbitration awards. If the claim is properly adjudicated and defended, none of the underlying issues can be further litigated and almost always, the award is upheld. Our first big case in Chengdu was this arbitration award. We were able to collect on that award. Our fee was contingent upon collection and this success justified our decision to open a branch office in China. Later on, we resolved a number of similar collection matters emanating from Chengdu.

* * * * * * * *

In Chengdu, we marketed to potential Chinese immigrants, local trademark companies, export companies, as well as Americans desirous of immigrating their Chinese spouses. It takes time to build a practice and a clientele, sometimes years. By the time I was in China, I was in my mid-forties. I had developed law offices in downtown Los Angeles and a satellite office in the San Gabriel Valley to serve the Chinese community. I also developed a practice in Riverside, the Inland Empire. The avenues for marketing to prospective clients were different in China. I made efforts to establish relationships with as many lawyers as possible. I met with local trademark firms, which hired us to file trademark and copyright applications in the United States. I visited import export companies, met many professionals in foreign trade and contacted trade organizations such as the China Chamber of International Commerce. I attended networking meetings, trying to get those interested in doing business with America to use our law firm. I went to bar association meetings. One such meeting was a large fundraiser of the Legal Aid Society where I met scores of local attorneys. Those lawyers took on cases *pro bono* involving Chengdu's less fortunate in need of legal help. As the only foreign law firm in town, we were expected to give a generous donation. We did our best.

I became familiar with manufacturers who sent products overseas. I gave seminars to these manufacturers. Every time I gave a seminar, whether it was in Chengdu or neighboring Dujiangyen or in other cities like Lijiang or Kuoming, I brought hundreds of the law firm's brochures. I would place a brochure on each seat in the seminar venue. I would receive calls as a result of distributing these brochures.

Since there is a United States Consulate in Chengdu, part of my job was to assist clients at the consulate with their visa processing needs. This involved trying to persuade a visa officer to permit the issuance of a visa when it was not obvious the visa should be granted. While in Chengdu, I received an email from my Los Angeles office that a Chinese multinational manager living in Arizona hired us to help her husband and son obtain a visa at the Chengdu Consulate. The multinational manager was in the United States on a valid L-1 visa (Non-Immigrant Visa for Multinational Transferee). The husband and son had been denied their L-2 visas (immediate family member of L-1 visa holder) based on the weak documentation they submitted to the visa officer. My Los Angeles office instructed the U.S. based client to send detailed documents, including corporate tax returns, profit and loss statements, and the company's business plan to the Chengdu office via priority mail. I received the documents and one evening met the husband and son in my Chengdu apartment. The son sat on my couch quietly as Zhen Long and I spoke to the husband. We spent several hours going over their records. In addition to the strength of the U.S. company, I sought to verify proof of the relationship of the two to the L-1 visa holder. The next day, I brought them to the consulate where we met with Mort Altman. After showing him the U.S. documents and valid evidence of the relationship, he approved the visa.

I met many people in Chengdu, as I was the only Western lawyer there. I acquired an extent of notoriety. Enjoying the life, I would have a beer or two with Chengdu friends at one of the Western style bars. At one such bar, the owner invited me to sit at a large table with a number of visiting foreigners. An elderly man stood, introducing himself as being from Austria. As he shook my hand, he said, *"Heil Hitler!"* My immediate instinct was to deck him, but he was elderly and I was in China. I thought if I punch this guy out and he dies, I would be prosecuted for murder. I restrained myself. I asked the woman, introduced as his wife, if he was serious. She said he was just being playful. I let it go, had a beer and guardedly listened to the man tell stories. When he started telling the story of his dog, Mussolini, I had enough. The owner followed me out. I mentioned the Japanese massacre of the Chinese in Nanjing during World War II. I told her that the customer's behavior was akin to a former Japanese soldier coming into her bar and bragging about how great it was raping and killing all those Chinese women.

* * * * * * * *

In 2001, China's long sought membership in the World Trade Organization (WTO) finally bore fruit. China became a member. The United States Embassy sponsored WTO seminars throughout China. For the area served by the Chengdu Consulate, they asked me to participate in these seminars. With members of the consulate, including the staff of the United States Foreign Commercial Service, I traveled to Kunming and Lijiang. I lectured on international trade agreements, intellectual property infringement and enforcement, including punishment for violations of commercial counterfeiting crimes in the United States. Since commercial counterfeiting is such a problem in China, I was told to concentrate my lecture mostly on this subject. As I had handled such cases throughout my career as a criminal defense attorney, I was particularly suited for these lectures.

In ancient Lijiang, there is a majestic mountain looming over the city called Snow Mountain. The people of Lijiang are especially proud of this mountain. I started my lecture to a very large group talking about how Snow Mountain is a treasure, how the water from Snow Mountain is delicious, so pure and natural. I suggested the city should contract with a beverage company to bottle the refreshing water and sell it in America as Snow Mountain Water. The people of Lijiang would make a fortune. How would they feel if someone in America used bottled tap water, put a picture of Snow Mountain on it, then sold it as crystal pure Snow Mountain Water? The buyers of the bottled water would be defrauded, thinking they were drinking genuine Snow Mountain water. And the people of Lijiang, whose mountain this is, would see no benefit. That would be unfair. Lijiang would be cheated and some criminal would be getting rich by stealing Lijiang's greatest asset. My lecture was designed to persuade the people of China to protect the intellectual property rights of others. Snow Mountain's water belonged to the citizens of Lijiang. The rights to distribute this unique resource should not be violated.

I was traveling from Los Angeles to Chengdu for ten days every two months. I did this for over three years, during which time my Chinese language skills improved. I had met many local attorneys, businessmen and expats living in Chengdu. I had a lengthy list of contacts there. The United States ambassador to China was an attorney from a huge law firm with offices in the Los Angeles Arco Towers. Our office at the time was also in the Arco Towers. The ambassador would hold Rule of Law (no one is above the law) conferences sponsored by the U.S. Consulate where local lawyers would be invited to take part in a discussion about the American legal system. The U.S. embassy is in Beijing and the four consulates are in Chengdu, Shanghai, Guangzhou and Shenyang. Prominent lawyers and judges from these areas would be invited to the respective consulate's event. Because U.S. consulate personnel knew about my Chengdu law office, they asked for my list of local attorneys, which I provided. There was a good crowd at the event. It was a lively, productive affair. Cocktails and hors d'oeuvres were served. I was introduced to the ambassador, whom I had never met. He held a plate of hors d'oeuvres in one hand while he shook my hand with the other, saying he thought I was very brave to open a branch law office in Chengdu. I thanked him, not really knowing if he was complimenting or ridiculing me. We talked about being lawyers, both of us having offices in the Arco

Towers. During our conversation, a few people came up, but mostly the two of us were talking face to face and eating hors d'oeuvres. At one point while the ambassador was speaking, a piece of food flew from his mouth and like a guided missile, plunged into my left eye. I tried to disregard it. I wanted to say, "Hey, man, you just spit a wad of food in my eye," but he was the ambassador and who was I to accuse him? My eye started tearing, both of us ignoring it. Finally I excused myself to go to the restroom.

* * * * * * * *

It was 2004, my twentieth year after becoming a member of the bar. Still wanting to grow my China business, I decided to spend a year in Shanghai, marketing legal services and exploring opportunities to open a second China office. From Shanghai, I could service the Chengdu office via a short 2½-hour domestic flight.

Jia-Ning and I rented an apartment in the Gubei area of Shanghai, on the corner of Hongqiao Lu and Shuicheng Lu, in an apartment complex called Miramar, across the street from the Carrefour Department Store. Jia-Ning liked the Gubei area of Shanghai, as she had many friends from Taipei living there. She even had friends living in Miramar. Fortuitously, this complex also housed the Shanghai Jewish Center.

Once we moved to Shanghai, I continued to market my law business. I spent time at the American Chamber of Commerce in Shanghai meeting Americans. I met many members of the Shanghai Jewish community, foreigners doing business in China who would often consult me on legal issues. At one point, a Silicon Valley company hired me to do their visa processing. I would occasionally meet clients in the office of a Shanghai lawyer, Brian Yang, a friend. We cooperated on various cases. Some of the cases where clients needed only a local lawyer, I simply referred to Brian. Some I would retain and help with immigration or business transactional needs. Some were Americans doing business in China, wishing to legalize their existing business in Shanghai with the appropriate licensing and permits.

For these clients, I would explain the three options to establish a foreign company in China. An American firm could launch a Foreign Representative Office, as my firm did. There is one problem with this type of business enterprise. The Foreign Representative Office can only market for the American domiciled business, and in those days, was not permitted to transact business on its own. Secondly, an American firm can establish a Joint Venture with a Chinese company, investing capital into the joint venture, but having to rely on the trustworthiness of the Chinese partner. Thirdly, an American firm can open a Wholly Owned Foreign Enterprise (WOFE). This has fewer restrictions than a Foreign Representative Office, and no reliance on the dependability of partners is required.

I flew back and forth to Chengdu. I also kept busy preparing for a complicated real estate fraud trial set to start in San Diego nine months after we had moved to Shanghai. The reports and exhibits on the case contained thousands of pages. Fortunately I had the pages on CD. The time I had away from the everyday grind of a courtroom allowed me time to study and prepare for this complex trial.

Shanghai is divided into two areas: Pudong, east of the Wangpu River and Puxi, west of the Wangpu. Pudong was built in the last two decades. Now, its skyline rivals any city in the world, with buildings like the Pearl Tower and the Jingma Office Building, enormous and futuristic structures. I tell people that Shanghai's contemporary skyline reminds me of the Jetson's cartoon I watched as a child. Jia-Ning and I had the best year of our lives in Shanghai.

We found schools for our children. Nathan, age eight, was enrolled in an international school and Noah, age four, attended a local bi-lingual school, the Tweety Bird School, named after the Warner Brothers' character with the bad lisp. How ironic, an English language school named after a cartoon character with English diction problems. We hired an *aiee*, a nanny who lived in a small room in our apartment. *Aiee* cared for the boys as if they were her own. The three were constant companions. One day I came home to an indoor baseball game. The boys were standing in the hallway of the apartment, Nathan near the bedroom, *Aiee* down the hall near the door. They were wearing baseball mitts and pitching a hard ball back and forth. I noticed the light switch next to *Aiee* was broken. There was a crack in the wall behind Nathan. They just kept on playing, the ball flying everywhere.

Aiee would accompany us on outings. We visited historical and cultural sites in Shanghai. Our older son's first language was Mandarin. Because his older brother, his best friend, only spoke English to him, our younger son would not speak Mandarin. Jia-Ning's attempts to speak Chinese resulted in his understanding, but he stubbornly refused to speak. After about two weeks with *Aiee*, he was fluent.

For the first time since our older son was born, we enjoyed our freedom. We explored the nightlife of Shanghai: karaoke, parties, restaurants, *Phantom of the Opera* at the Shanghai Theater and museums. Jia-Ning is masterful at finding intriguing places to go. We befriended many interesting people, and after several weeks, received phone calls from strangers informed that Jia-Ning knew Shanghai better than anyone. I continued studying Mandarin, even had a tutor for a short time. While living in Shanghai, I was able to communicate in Chinese on an everyday basis.

After nine months in Shanghai, I returned to Southern California. With co-counsel and friend Ben Jacobson, I defended my client on the real estate fraud trial in San Diego, living for a month in a hotel room. My wife and children remained in Shanghai. In San Diego, my cell phone constantly rang, clients asking me: "Where have you been? I need your help. Can't you represent me on my criminal case?" As much as I enjoyed Shanghai, I realized I missed my practice in the United States. After the trial, I flew back to Shanghai. We stayed the remainder of the year, closed up shop and returned home. I resumed my practice in the United States, but this time I did it alone, without a partner. It was 2005 and I hit the ground running.

* * * * * * * *

Serving the local San Gabriel Valley community, I had a client list that often included well known Chinese defendants. My cases were closely followed by the Chinese media. I became a source for crime reporters seeking expert commentary on legal matters, and was quoted regularly in Mandarin language newspapers. My caseload reached capacity and I was working all the time.

It is difficult for lawyers to get away. Whenever I plan a vacation, I am retained by a new client in an emergency situation. Criminal lawyers are usually contacted when the client is in urgent need. Either he is in jail or his court date is fast approaching. After several years without a vacation, I arranged for a family tour of Israel over the winter holidays,

2007. We were at the airport when my cell phone rang. A local Chinese newspaper reporter asked me for a comment about the thirty-two sex workers arrested the previous night in the San Gabriel Valley. I had not heard about it, but gave a standard comment on this type of case: "The police are often overzealous in these investigations, and go to great lengths and expense to try to expose low-level, misdemeanor sexual conduct." Then my phone started ringing like crazy. Other reporters and potential clients were calling while we were in line waiting to board a plane to Tel Aviv. I had committed to going to Israel, even if it meant I would lose potential clients. I would be away for ten days.

We arrived in the middle of the night at Tel Aviv's Ben Gurion Airport. Jia-Ning requested that I ask the shuttle driver the time. I had diligently studied Hebrew as a youth. I started to ask the driver for the time in Hebrew and my words came out in Chinese. Jia-Ning thought it hysterical. After several days in Israel, Jia-Ning and the boys craved Chinese food. We were waiting to meet a friend for dinner at a Tel Aviv Chinese restaurant. A Chinese woman came from the kitchen area and asked me something in Hebrew. I said in Hebrew, *"Ani lo midaber evrete."* (I do not speak Hebrew.) I asked in Hebrew, *"At midebaret englit?"* (Do you speak English?) She said no. Then I asked in Chinese, *"Ni jiang guoyu, ma?"* (Do you speak Chinese?) She did. We communicated in Chinese, Jia-Ning doing most of the talking.

For ten days, we toured. We saw the ancient ruins of Masada, the famous mountain fortress overlooking the Dead Sea, where Jewish zealots resisted the Romans for seven years. Eventually, the Romans built a ramp, climbing the side of the mountain to overtake the Jewish garrison. Nine hundred sixty Jews committed mass suicide rather than be enslaved by the attacking Romans. There is a national attitude that the People of Israel would fight to the death rather than be enslaved again. My sons floated on the Dead Sea, where high salt content prevents a swimmer from sinking. We went to the Wailing Wall in Jerusalem, where I wore tefillin (phylacteries), black leather straps and boxes, containing Torah verses, fixed on my head and wrapped around my left arm. The eminent twelfth-century Jewish scholar Maimonides taught: "Great is the sanctity of tefillin, for as long as the tefillin are upon man's head and arm, he is humble." When I was young, I was instructed how to wear tefillin.

We toured the beaches of Tel Aviv, the cities of Jerusalem and Haifa. We stayed in a kibbutz in Northern Israel, sandwiched between Lebanon and Syria. We saw the Golan Heights, where we watched UN security forces at the border between Syria and Israel. We visited the Ba'hai Temple with its lush gardens. We marveled at Acre, an ancient port city, the largest during the Roman rule. We viewed Caesarea, built by King Herod. We toured Yad Vishem, Israel's Holocaust museum. After ten days, we came home. Back to work, I was swamped with a caseload that had been neglected. This trip with my family was much different from an earlier trip to Israel.

At the age of eighteen, Solomon Rose and I attended an Ulpan in Israel, a learning program for Hebrew and Israeli culture. We stayed in Haifa for the summer. We were in Haifa during the Israeli commando raid in Entebbe, Uganda. The raid of Entebbe was called Operation Thunderbolt. Its purpose was to rescue one hundred hostages from the Popular Front for the Liberation of Palestine. Operation leader Yonatan Netanyahu was killed, as were three hostages and forty-five soldiers under the command of the dictator of Uganda, Idi-Amin. This raid and its relative success was a source of great pride to Israelis.

While Solomon and I were wandering around checking out local culture, we returned to our group too late for dinner. We were hungry. Across the street from our lodging was an apple orchard, where we climbed a fence and picked about ten apples for dinner. It never occurred to us that we were stealing. We just saw apple trees and thought we would eat a few apples. As we were leaving, a thin, middle-aged, swarthy man drove up, pointed his machine gun at us, pushed the nozzle into my lower back and ordered us into his car. He drove us to the headquarters of the kibbutz, which owned the orchard. A kibbutz is a communal farm. They scolded us, calling us thieves. They told us the police were coming and that we would spend the rest of our trip in an Israeli jail. Solomon sat patiently. I was angry that the guard had shoved the machine gun into my back. I told them that I had a right to talk to U.S. Consular Officials and demanded a phone to call the United States Embassy. They were surprised and did not know if, as an American citizen, I had a right to such a call. After heated argument, they softened. We apologized, explaining we realized our action was an act of theft. We had not thought about this in moral terms. Of course, from a historical perspective, Solomon and I were not the first men to be punished for eating the forbidden fruit in the Holy Land. Finally, they released us. We were disoriented and did not know exactly where we were. We arrived back late that night after walking around in circles. In my recent family trip to Israel, Jia-Ning purchased some fruit outside our hotel. I could not bring myself to eat the apples.

Afterword

I continue to practice criminal and immigration law. I ran into an old friend, Freddy Bocelli, a criminal defense lawyer in West Covina. I told him my story. He smiled: "Sandy, where else but in America can a Jewish kid from Detroit marry a Chinese woman visiting Los Angeles, practice law in China, move to Shanghai, come back to Los Angeles and maintain a practice with predominantly Chinese clients? Where else but in America?"

Recently, I received a phone call from a young Chinese man, who said he was looking through the Chinese Yellow Pages and saw my picture. He told his American girlfriend that I saved him from a hard life in China and that when he was a child, he had come to my house with his father and met with me regarding their visa processing the next day at the Chengdu Consulate. I remembered the eleven-year-old boy who sat on my couch while I talked with his father. His American girlfriend doubted his story, that this Caucasian lawyer in the Chinese Yellow Pages had at one time lived in Chengdu and that her boyfriend, at the age of eleven, was in the lawyer's Chengdu home. I promised I would tell his girlfriend the truth. A couple days later, he came to my office with his girlfriend. I told her the story. Two weeks later, he called again and referred a friend in need of legal help.

Connected by thousands of invisible cords, life goes on in the busy law offices of Sanford H. Perliss.

Acknowledgements

Writing my book has been a collaborative process. I'm most grateful for all the help. It's been a fascinating endeavor to create a literary and stimulating conversation. My collaborators have made the work fun and have both challenged and encouraged me along the sometimes rocky roads of written expression. I want to extend my thanks to all who have read *A Thousand Invisible Cords*. It means so much to have someone say that they've enjoyed the reading. I appreciate and benefited from excellent suggestions from my friends and family to improve the book. Writing about my life and career helped me connect to both long-time and new friends. I hope if any bad feelings arose in the process that they will be healed with time and good laughs.

My deep appreciation to: My editor Morgan Zo Callahan, Albert Grana, Michael Schechter, Gary Schouborg, Scott Wood, James Won, Susie Ling, Amanda Wang, Sam Haycraft, Steve Kramer, Joel Isaacson, Tony Meyers, Vivian Tan, Lee Mitchell, Jeff Kozono, Michael Pearl, Anthony Robusto, my parents Sallie and Bob Perliss and my sister Cindy Keller.

Contact information: sperliss@perlisslaw.com
www.perlisslaw.com
1-626-300-8688